IN HIS
PRESENCE

No matter what I do
Be it all for gain or loss
I'll paint the world to You
and stand behind the cross

Elaine Rose
2019

ISBN 978-1-64569-676-6 (paperback)
ISBN 978-1-64569-678-0 (hardcover)
ISBN 978-1-64569-677-3 (digital)

Christian Faith Publishing, Inc.
832 Park Avenue
Meadville, PA 16335
www.christianfaithpublishing.com

Printed in the United States of America

*E*very morning, I make an early pilgrimage to the deck, to fill a couple of shallow pans with sunflower seeds, not a particularly striking sight in my tattered old yellow bathrobe, and I haven't looked in the mirror yet, can't say that I want to, but nonetheless, it is breakfast time for my feathered friends and my one faithful squirrel. I slip into a pair of old white clogs that are higher on my feet than the inches of snow that still graces the deck floor, and out I go. Not really paying any particular attention to my surroundings, I heard the most beautiful bird song this morning, totally unexpected as the blue jays don't really sing but instead do a lot of squawking. I stopped in my tracks; this song was so pretty. I have no idea what kind of bird it was, but I will be mindful to watch the feeder all day to see if someone new comes for a visit. In an instant, the surroundings change, and I needed to hear that song today. Listening and looking for the beauty that surrounds us in the midst of the chaos of this world. What a wonderful way to start the day. My smile goes all the way through to my heart. Thank you, Father, for eyes that see, ears that hear, and a heart that loves.

$\mathcal{W}$e hopped into the buggy to head east from the mountains yesterday morning and didn't realize the temperature had taken such a steep nosedive during the wee early hours of the morning. In other words, there was ice, not just frost on the windshield. We had gotten up early and ate a quick breakfast and hit the ground ready to roll. Well in a little bit. The windshield needed to thaw, and that was going to take a few more than five minutes. No amount of running the windshield washers or using the washer fluid was going to magically dissolve the ice, and there was no sunrise to watch just yet, so we sat there. The longer I watched the frosty ice thaw intrigued with the slow process of melting, I couldn't help but think of folks that seem to be a lot like that windshield, frozen over, yet with a gentle amount of warmth and some sincere tender loving kindness, they too begin to lose their icy crust. Wonder why people freeze up so hard? Is it a defense mechanism? They've been hurt before and are wary of letting anyone see their soft spot. Difficult people will often warm with a little patience and a whole lot of his amazing love, so if you run into someone with a frosty exterior today, try a little kindness and sincerity, some genuine love, and I will bet eventually you may see a little warmth begin to glow, not in every case but in a lot. In our crazy world, people just need us to care, to be available, and to love first, because that is what we are supposed to do.

*A*nother year is about over. Did you do better this year? Learn something new, stretch your imagination, and care and give a little more? Maybe it was a tough year, full of new challenges, tragic loss, situations that pulled you under? Come with me for just a moment. Step outside the front door into the stillness of the morning here in the country. All is quiet. No sound. No wind. No birds awake yet. Take a deep breath. The air is cold, and it will refresh you. Look up at the sky. There are stars twinkling as they have been for many years. Stand and rest in the silence. Sometimes it takes a few moments of quiet, to find yourself again, away from all the technology and the entertainment that we find in this world that flows by our eyes at a rapid pace. When your soul is quiet, listen to your heart. You might hear from your Maker, and just maybe he would like for you to talk to him. A new year looms ahead. Stay in touch. When you feel you've lost your center, come back to that quiet moment. It bears repeating. May you find peace and be refreshed as we prepare to start a new calendar year. Time to raise the faith a bar or two. All is well, and he is in control no matter what others tell you.

*T*he courtroom was humming with quiet speculation. People spoke in hushed tones waiting for the day's events to unfold. The back door opened, the room fell silent, and the criminal and his lawyer walked in. Within a few minutes, the judge was behind the bench, and the gavel dropped. Closing arguments ensued. Even the criminal's family knew he was guilty, yet they prayed for a light sentence.

What he had done was unthinkable. The jury had come to their decision, and juror number one stepped forward to deliver the verdict. Guilty as charged. The criminal sat with his head down. No emotion. All of a sudden, a man stood in the midst of the crowd and asked to approach the bench.

"Your honor, I would like to take the punishment for this man. I have known him for years. And yes, he is guilty, but I care about his welfare. I will take his place."

Gasps escaped from the startled crowd, the judge tried not to stare, and the criminal's shoulders began to fold. Sound a little far-fetched? A little difficult to wrap your head around? Why would someone, who was totally innocent, ever take the punishment for a person that barely acknowledged his presence? Yes, hard to believe. We can't even fathom this kind of love. Pick up the good book and scan the pages sometime. This scenario isn't so unbelievable. Hard to imagine, but very real. Nonetheless, how do you feel about taking the blame for an evil someone else did that you had no part in? The kind of love that says no matter what you and I do that is so terribly wrong, our heavenly Father forgives us. His Son stepped forward and took our punishment so we don't have to. And there is eternal life ahead for us if we will just confess our belief. You are loved and forgiven. Faith in action. Time to be a little more than grateful.

*W*hat makes a person, or something you use, dependable? Is it their last name, the area of the country they come from, or their handshake? Or maybe you use a certain brand or product, a referral from someone else, or the same brand you've used for years? Sometimes these days, I wonder if you can find dependability anywhere anymore? The folks I vote for after they get into office seem to have a habit of doing a three sixty on their campaign promises. The brand of washing machine I bought last time, which is supposed to be reliable, has survived three years and is about done. What about us? How do you and I measure up in the dependability department? One of the first lessons we learned when our path through parenthood started was that if you say you are going to do something, you had better follow-through. Those little people know when you are sincere and when you are about to just slough your promise off. They don't take being disappointed lightly. A very good lesson for life. If you are traveling a rocky road, and feel like you are all alone, that no one cares about the struggles you are negotiating, take heed, there is one who is always dependable and would love to hear from you. We may not always understand his timing, but do not be dismayed. He has heard your voice, and he has never left anyone in a lurch. Trust His word. You can depend on it. May you and I be the same kind of people, those who follow through and any one can depend on.

*T*hey said to him, "Lord, we want our eyes to be opened."

The decree rang out across the living room early Saturday morning that this was the day to remove the room air conditioners from the bedroom windows and store them for the winter. Not a problem, and putting the storm windows back in would help keep the utility costs down this winter, and that's always a good thing. The air conditioners were removed without a hitch and stored, but the words that stunned me next were, "I need to wash one of these windows." Gasps.

Very happy to oblige, I gathered a bucket with soapy water and all the cleaning supplies the lineman would need. I'm too short to do this job, so his help was very much appreciated. He washed the outside of the grimy window, and I washed the inside. We were totally blown way with the scenery. I'm not sure how windows get layers of dirt on them, but in the country with the dust and beetles' residue, it's not too hard to figure out. Layer upon layer of dirt was removed, some of it took some hard scrubbing, and the rest was easily washed away. All of this dirt had accumulated slowly over time, not overnight, and had to be removed little at a time. Makes me wonder about the windows I look though in my soul. I try to ask for forgiveness moment by moment, but sometimes the wrongs accumulate and layer up and begin to dull the way we react and see things. We don't realize it because it happens so gradually. Sometimes a good cleaning opens our eyes and our hearts. It's a continual process. You might just be surprised at all the details your eyes envision with the lenses clear. Let him clean your windows, and you will see clearly now.

*A*fter the long journey back to the flat lands of the Midwest, we crawled in between the covers, totally exhausted.

Ahh, the familiar mattress and pillow. Yet for some reason, this just didn't feel as comfortable as I remembered. Hmmm, and then it dawned on me. We had been gone to the mountains longer than usual this summer. And as we laid there, we realized that this wasn't as homey as we remembered. And I began to ponder, the longer I am here in this world, the less it feels like home. I think in educational circles this is referred to as "transitioning," or maybe I'm just getting old. And I ponder "if" those who have gone on before me felt the same way? From a little child facing the future, the future isn't quite what I expected. Don't get me wrong, we are blessed beyond measure and love living wherever we are and will continue to work until that day that we're done. Maybe even right up until noon on the day of our funerals we know we're not "home" yet. When we are finished with his work here on earth, a better home, our final home, is waiting, and we don't even have to try to imagine what it will be like as we can't grasp what waits for us that he has prepared. I just know we want to go there. And in the infamous word of our favorite "in box" road guide, you have reached your final destination. Enter into the joy of the Lord. His presence that we long for, forever, sounds like a really nice place to settle in.

*H*ave you got your eye on a new craft, skill, or casserole that you want to try? Feeling a bit adventurous about a biking trip or snorkeling? Are you all lined out and ready to go? What did you do first? Did you consult the information highway, buy a book, or watch a video or two? You've made the decision that a new skill set looks inviting and you are ready to just do it. Have you got your equipment lined out and everything you need and maybe a guide to get you started? What about your mind? Is your mind-set solid and your confidence level good? Sounds like you are all set. If we spend this amount of time preparing to do something new, how much more time should we commit to our relationships, especially with our Maker? After we lift up a thankful word for waking us up another day, maybe it would be a good idea to also ask him to renew our minds and place a right spirit in our thinking. Taking captive the thoughts that threaten to pull us down or wouldn't be pleasing to him. If we want good outcomes no matter what we put our hands to, we need solid guidance and preparation, and hopefully our relationship with the one who love us most isn't a fly by thought. It is a forever relationship. It takes a bit of work, but, oh, the rewards. Starting the day with him and heaven, and our minds keeping his will front and center. The best way to start a new week and new day, any time. Refresh my mind, Lord.

*S*top for just a minute and think about the first sound you heard this morning. Was it the alarm clock, the coffee maker turning on, or the quiet hum of the refrigerator? Sounds that we hear all the time and that we take for granted until the electricity goes off or we have stopped up ears from a cold or something else. We live in a noisy world. Do you ever take time to step outside when the wind is calm and just listen? You will probably hear some farm equipment in the distance this time of year, or if the wind has kicked up, you might hear the traffic on a nearby interstate. Are there certain voices that you love to hear? Your mom or dad's quiet voice, the sound of a child, a dear friend? Have you taken the time lately to listen to your Maker's voice? We get so busy, and taking time to really listen is a commodity we don't allow ourselves very often. And when we do talk to our Maker, many times it is a please do list. This is my agenda. Please follow through, and off to the daily race we go. Maybe for just a moment, it would be wise for us to offer our praise and thanksgiving, and then just be quiet for a moment and let him have a word. That still small voice that offers encouragement, an answer to a prayer that you have been waiting for, a suggestion that you need to take care of something that is bothering Him. I am so thankful that my Maker allows me to talk to him, and he hears me when I call on him. And today I'm reminded that I need to remain quiet and let him do some talking likewise. Putting on our listening ears, being aware of his voice, and recognizing his voice. Something to be thankful for every day.

*N*ot long after we moved to this area, I was wishing for a piano. In our early married life, I had a big old upright, and it was so heavy and hard to move that it didn't come with us. So I kept my ear to the ground so to speak, in hopes that one day a piano would become available. It wasn't long until a pastor that was moving had to part with his piano, and I bought his piano from him. The piano is beautiful and solid, a concert spinet, and I was delighted in it from the first day it was in the house, and it sounded good. Over the years, it has been played a lot, by many folks, some learning to play on that bench. Seasons come and go, and slowly the piano began to lose its tune. And then about a year ago, I realized how badly it sounded when played. You could still make out the songs, and sometimes it would even appear to mend the sour notes and correct the tune, but it was a long way from sounding perfect. The music was kind of muffled and heavy. After much research, I found a gentleman who tunes pianos and has an amazing background in music. He uses the piano tuning fork to repair the distorted sounds, so I enlisted his help. He spent a couple of hours working on the piano and bringing it back into tune. And when he finished working on it, I was dumbstruck. This precious piano had never sounded so good, even when I brought it home the first day. The music emanating from the piano is now crisp and on tune. The sounds are rich and full, and it truly is a pleasure to sit on the bench and play. Quite a transformation.

Like us, life wears us down, and sometimes we become a little out of tune and sour, and our thoughts are heavy. We acquire some habits that we shouldn't have or thoughts that really aren't good, and sometimes we have to hit rock bottom to realize the awful condition we are in and have allowed ourselves to become. Like the piano man, who tunes and tweaks, we have a Maker that is so much more capable of putting us back in tune, who is capable of eradicating the sour notes. The broken pieces of us come back together if we are willing. He truly is the repairman for all the we need, and if we have slipped away from him, he welcomes us back. If the song you are singing is a bit off key today, or maybe you've lost your melody, he waits for your return, and he won't disappoint you. A new song to sing awaits.

*A*bout this time of year, every year, we are inundated with a variety of award shows that are going to be televised. Some are creating quite a buzz this year, and frankly, I could care less. I don't look to Hollywood to entertain me, and yes, I enjoy a movie once in a while. If it doesn't catch me in ten minutes when the movie starts, and the same goes for books, I'm up and gone. That said, I'm just not a follower of the big screen, which brings me to a question. I wonder why we crave awards so much? Competition seems to be part of us since the beginning of time, starting with two brothers vying for status and being chosen the favorite of their father. I wonder somewhere back in caveman time if somebody threw a rock and challenged the next guy to throw it farther. Is that where all of this came from? Competition for the best cake, the best dance, the sharpest dog, the longest touchdown pass and on it goes so that awards may be won. Why are we not content to just do our best and be satisfied with our own personal accomplishment at whatever we are doing? Look at me. Look at me. Does it come from not getting the attention we crave as children, the yearning to be acknowledged? I could chase this subject around until I land on the moon yet may never know exactly why we need statues, medals, and kudos. So I'll continue on doing my best and being satisfied with that. At this point in my life, all I want to hear is well done good and faithful servant. Applause from my Maker in heaven. The best!

"And I am certain that God, who began a good work in you, will carry it on to completion until it is finally finished on the day when Christ Jesus returns."

Looking around my house, I have several projects that have been started with the greatest fervor that haven't been finished. I started each project with great gusto and admirable intentions, but somewhere along the line, I derailed and got sidetracked, and my projects went by the wayside, and every so often, I get back on track, and the work on these projects begin again, and before I know it, life's interruptions bring my good intentions to a smashing halt again. I have made plans that after the holiday season is over, I will set aside a devoted amount of time each day to work on these projects, so we will see how it goes. There are days that I feel like a scarecrow that is losing its stuffing to the wind, and there are empty spots where there once was straw for stuffing, and I honestly wonder what my Maker has in store for me, but a little more time in his word and talking to him, I find myself somewhat put back together. How refreshing it is to have the above verse to fall back on when I begin to question those why am I here questions. And what on earth am I supposed to be doing? I take comfort in knowing that I am a work in progress. There are some scars and a few tender bruises. The ears don't hear as well as they once did, and the eyes need help, but what a joy to know that all my imperfections will be completed and made whole the way they are supposed to be when I stand before him. If you belong to him, he has big plans for you, and there is coming a day when those plans will be completed. That's encouragement. His word is solid.

Traveling life's journey can seem like the tallest of mountain climbs sometimes, and one thing I've discovered is the most cumbersome thing to carry on this journey is a heavy heart. Hurting for those who have illness, broken relationships, family loss, and addiction problems that seem insurmountable. That heavy heart can almost weigh you down clear to the ground. Don't ignore friends who offer to help you. They might be blessed by helping out. And don't' be afraid to ask for help. You would help your friends just the same. We don't have to travel alone; there is help closer and quicker than a phone call away. He knows what matters to you, and he knows how badly you are hurting. Don't be afraid to ask for strength and comfort. He is waiting in the most quiet whisper. He hears and answers. Trust his heart.

*P*erfume and incense bring joy to the heart, and the pleasantness of a friend springs from their heartfelt advice.

I love happy endings, and I especially enjoy watching the videos of our servicemen and women coming home and then surprising their family members. Whether they pop out of a box, or whatever, yes, it makes me cry, but they are happy tears. Do you have a memory of getting to see someone you haven't seen for a long time and the emotions you felt? Running into the house after the first day of school to tell your mom all about your day or awaiting a longtime friend's arrival and the joy you feel getting to pick up where you left off with that friend? The feeling is kind of hard to describe, your heart feels like it is going to burst, and you can't talk fast enough. I'm not sure I can even imagine what it is going to be like to walk through the golden gates of heaven. First into the arms of my Maker but then to see my loved ones who have gone on before that I haven't seen for so long. To have my heavenly Father say welcome home. I can hardly imagine, and I have a feeling my imagination doesn't touch the tip of the iceberg. A good reminder that we need to plan ahead—we don't just die and land in heaven without making arrangements, knowing you are going home, when this life is over. Well done, faithful one, well done.

*T*here is an art form that I participate in that will make you wonder about my sanity if you don't already. Quilting, the art of taking perfectly good pieces of fabric and slicing and dicing them and sewing them back together. I'll have to admit, it seems rather redundant. There is a challenge in trying to get tiny triangles and squares to line up to make just the right design whether you are following a pattern or just free handing it. And no matter how careful you are cutting and sewing, at some time, there will be a do over. Just when you've squared all the corners and lined the fabric into position, for no apparent reason, you may find your stitching is off one way or another, and the seam ripper will become your dreaded friend. And after you have removed the stitches, there will still be a slight echo on the fabric where you have sewn, and removing stitches from a fabric with a nap such as flannel will give you nightmares for days to come. A whole lot like life. No matter how careful you are and how straight you shoot, no matter how many plans you have laid in stone, there will be times when you have to start over. Just when you think everything is ready for smooth sailing, there will be a storm. If you aren't one to be flexible and adjust your plans according to life as it happens, you are probably going to be miserable. Flat tires happen when going on vacation. Being laid off from a job that you love isn't pleasant. Getting the flu is never fun but especially tough when you had plans for a movie night. So it goes. The storms come in all sizes too, from the small to the tall. Next time your plans don't quite line up, consult your owner's manual and the writer's words. You will find some gems that will help you cope with the crooked seams of life, learning to adjust my sails and seams.

*Y*esterday, I ran into one of those invisible walls that you just don't see coming, and then it stops you in your tracks for a while. Imagine, for just a moment, spending hours preparing a business presentation that you know is going to propel your company forward by leaps and bounds. You turn the computer on, and the slideshow begins. Your excitement can barely be contained, and about halfway through the presentation, your boss says shut it off. This will never fly. Or maybe a family member asks you to come help unravel a situation that is about to take them under. You put on your best game face and have all of the top-notch advice ready to give, and when you arrive at their home, you are met at the door and dismissed as they have the problem solved and your services are no longer needed. So you head back home. Feels a bit like rejection in both instances, and it hurts the heart when you have help to give, but it is not received on any level.

How often are we guilty of plowing ahead trying to fix the broken things in our life without giving a thought to accepting the help of our Maker? We go racing ahead and go over the cliff, climb back up hurting all over, and we have the audacity to wonder where our Maker was and why he didn't stop us from taking the tumble we took?

Our sailboat lost air and ran aground and propelled us head first into the sand with a thud. So while we are dressing our wounds and wondering why we didn't have a divine intervention, he is shaking his head wondering why we didn't ask for help. We have a free will to do whatever we want, and when we start down the road on our own, we are on our own. There are going to be times when our most valiant offer of help is rejected.

Try to imagine how he must've felt all those years he walked the face of the earth and tried to help his fellow man. Three steps forward, five back, ready to try again. I'm forging ahead, this time asking for his help, and if I hit another wall today, it's not going to hurt so badly, because he is right there beside me.

$\mathcal{W}$e are a "hearing" challenged family for a variety of reasons, health, age, and work-related problems, yet there is something I've noticed just recently. Because we don't hear so well, in order to talk to one another, we have to make some concentrated effort to look at each other face-to-face and really listen which isn't all that bad. There are still times we play the selective hearing card but not as often anymore. None of us like to holler at each other, and we prefer using a normal volume on our conversations. So it just takes a little more work. That goes for listening too. We are paying close attention to one another to get the gist of what is being said, lest we misconstrue words and hear sentences that make no sense whatsoever, which can be quite comical at times. A good reminder that your Maker may be trying to get your attentions to tell you something important, and you need to have your listening ears on. He won't compete with the day-to-day noise that is so prevalent in our world. If you want to talk to him and seek him out, you may need to turn the volume down on your end of the conversation and just be still and listen. Who knows, you might just learn something. His words are the best.

This past weekend, I was reading and came across a story from the Old Testament that made me smile. I'm not sure I had ever read this story, and if I did, I didn't take time to let it soak in. The story is of a king that appears to have faced some difficulties being king, yet he knew where his help and success came from. He got the message. Sort of a Houston we have a problem here of an army coming to destroy him and his kingdom. Yet with that same message came the words that he would not have to fight the battle that was ahead. This king hit the ground on his knees with all the folks that lived close by and worshipped the Lord and gave thanks for all he was about to do. When it was time to go to battle, the king reminded his warriors to stand strong and keep the faith because they were going to be delivered. He also sent a few men ahead of this army to sing praises to their Maker and keeper of their backs. Kind of an unusual battle strategy, but it worked. The Lord remembered their faithfulness to him and caused such a frenzy in the opposing forces that they started fighting each other, and by the time our army coming to conquer arrived, everyone was dead. A pretty good lesson for us. When we are unsure what lies ahead for us, remain faithful and true to our Maker. Stand strong because he knows what is at the end of the dark hallway of our lives. No matter how confusing our circumstances are or how scary, if we can stay close to him, he will bring us through, and maybe when we are about to give way to the fear and uncertainty that lies ahead, we should sing. Sing often, and with each passing song, we might find that we grow stronger. Make a joyful noise to the Lord. Watch the darkness flee.

*W*e sat silently in the hospital room, late in the afternoon, and the busyness of the day was subsiding. There was very little noise whirling in the hallways outside our door. We were both prepared for the worst yet hopeful for a good report. Yet another doctor and we were hopeful for a strategy to at least lessen the pain in my daughter's knees. She's made of strong stuff, carries on as if nothing is wrong, yet the pain in her knees brings her to tears occasionally and makes her right down mad. She gets up and goes to work, cares for her friends, and loves her Maker.

Surely this time would be different, and we would have some hope to hang our hats on when we left the hospital, but there was no good news. Pretty much what we expected, and I, for one, was deflated. As we stepped in to the dusk of the evening, she let out a whoop. Bone on bone, baby! Just like my Nana and I had to laugh, not quite what I was expecting as I was about to dissolve into a puddle of tears. I'm not sure anything hurts a parent more than watching your child in pain and being helpless to fix it. We live in such a "fix it right now" society, and if it can't be fixed, we get a new whatever. Doesn't matter your social status, your affiliations, or the thickness of your billfold when you can't do anything about the pain your child is suffering, and in the perspective of medical problems, this was small stuff. There are those going through far worse.

In the meantime, we are trusting. We are hopeful. We are thankful for solutions and answers that are yet to be found, and we remain faithful to our Maker for what he enables us to do daily. It may stretch the elastic on our faith at times, but we'll keep going. He holds hope within our reach, and we're grabbing on. How sad it would be to not have him to walk beside us, to carry us through whatever trials come our way. How sad he would be if we didn't ask him for strength and help. If you are struggling today with tough circumstances or pain that are threatening to pull you under, you have a direct line to the one who is able to equip you and see you through. Call on him. He will answer.

*D*id you escape Monday unscathed? Rest assured, we all hit a few wrong chords, sing the wrong note, use the incorrect word in a sentence, or pick the wrong color paint. It is alright. All is not lost. Don't throw the baby out with the bath. All of us get caught in the trenches of life at times; it's how we climb back out that matters. Don't let your imperfections keep you from trying to do whatever it is you enjoy just because you were off a bit. We are all human, and mistakes will be made whether we like it or not.

Back on your feet. A new day awaits. Ask him to help you improve the song you have to sing or play. Pick a better color of paint. Write a better sentence. You have a second chance at a do over if your eyes are open. Being humbly grateful for another day. This is a cause for celebration.

*I*n a small rural community, Friday nights in the fall are pretty much all about eight-man football. And if you have lived in the community very long, you will probably know at least half the players on the home team, and you will recognize some of the names from the opposing team most likely. Attending one of these games is more than just a fun evening. It is supporting the team, their parents, the school, and the community. What could be better than showing up for our future? This past Friday night, we attended one of the games, and our team was really struggling the first half of the game, and I began to wonder if we all were going home very sad. Just seemed like none of their regular plays were working and the score wasn't in our favor. The second half started a little slow, but within a few minutes, one of our players intercepted a play from the opposing team, and the onlookers on the bleachers came to life and on their feet. It was as if I was sitting beside a red hot skillet of popcorn beginning to pop with no lid, and popcorn was popping out of the skillet all over everywhere. The crowd got loud, and all of a sudden supporting the kids was the name of the game. Then the same scenario happened three more times, and people were running up and down the sideline, jumping into the air, whooping and hollering. The score didn't reflect our success when we left the game, but we had won the second half, not just as a team but as a community. Isn't this the way we are supposed to be acting when one among us struggles and then all of a sudden makes vivid progress? Shouldn't we be fist pumping and shouting congratulations. Are you winning your struggles? We are all a part of the family of God, and we should be encouraging one other on and pulling for one another. Sadly I am guilty of thinking.

Well whoever or whatever circumstance doesn't affect me. They have family that can handle this, and I'll stay away.

Does anything feel better than a friend beside you when the going gets tough? You don't have to take up residence in their pocket to show that you care and are there to encourage them. A beautiful reminder of being engaged with those around you, sincerely caring about their lives, the good and the bad.

Cheer from the sidelines. Walk beside them. Do whatever it takes to help those around you get back on their feet, because he instructed us to do so.

*F*irst thing after my feet hit the floor in the morning, I grabbed a cup of coffee and headed to the computer for a quick check-in. I sit my coffee mug to the side of the computer and have a swallow here and there as I'm perusing all the news that is news, paying little attention to what is going on around my coffee mug. I then flipped the computer switch off and headed back to the kitchen to get the day started. Yesterday as I took a sip of coffee heading back into the kitchen, I was startled as there was something in my coffee that I had not seen, and it was in my mouthful of coffee. Oh, yuck. One of those nasty ladybug clones. I spit and spewed worse than a three-year-old with a mouth full of bubble gum-flavored antibiotic. Left a really bad taste in my mouth. I proceeded to pour what was left of my coffee down the drain lest I swallow a crunchy arm, leg, or toes, and then refilled my cup. My dad would always make the comment that someone or something that he didn't agree with or think was quite right. "Left a bad taste in his mouth."

Kind of like my ladybug clone left a nasty taste in my mouth, and then I think about all the things I do or say that are so wrong and wonder if they leave a bad taste in my heavenly Father's mouth? He must be so disappointed in me when I can do better. Today I will try to do better to put a filter over my mouth and double-check my actions before I take action or speak, filtering on. "Your statutes are my heritage forever. They are the joy of my heart."

I walked into the long white building. Three rows of six-foot tables spanned the width. Around the perimeter of the building sat assorted pieces of furniture. And the tables? They were filled with a lifetime's accumulation of everything you need to make a house a home. Some of the items were like new, others had been used until the shine was worn off, quilts and blanket were piled high, and an antique high chair and baby bed were in the mix. All that's left behind. My neighbors no longer reside down the road from us but have left us for someplace better, no pain, no sadness, no everyday trials. They were two of a kind, very proud, had started their married life with very little, and worked hard to provide for themselves. Independent? That's an understatement. Wouldn't ask for help unless they had no other choice. Giving? They shared some of the best beef we've ever eaten. Their code of ethics was high, and they were respected because of it.

Right was right, and wrong was wrong, and you'd better believe it. Which brings me to ask, what are you planning on leaving behind when your time on earth is done? Is the world a better place because you've lived here? Are you leaving it better than when you arrived?

We should all take a lesson. The artifacts and collectibles we leave will find new places in other homes, some with friends, others with total strangers. People that know nothing about us. I hope the memories that we leave behind will be more important. Loyalty, dependability, honesty, and loving, character traits that honor our Maker. He put us here for a reason, touching lives because he told us to, working on memories that count today.

*W*e live in a brick house and are very well insulated from noise. We just don't always hear what's going on outside, and it has to be a significant sound to catch our attention. As I was walking through the house one day last week, I stopped in my tracks to listen to a noise that was growing louder by the second. And then I recognized the sound. The snow geese were heading our way to find the morning's breakfast table in a nearby cornfield as they do every fall. The sky was full of these birds; all were following the leader and taking turns leading, wings beating to keep the airflow moving for all, working together to arrive at their destination. I didn't grow up in this area, and I am still in awe of these birds. They literally stop me in my tracks when I hear them.

The instinct that brings them from way up north to way down south to find food during the year is amazing. They are pretty well tuned by their Maker, and occasionally one gets shot or injured and falls from the sky. Yet the flock keeps moving on, doing what they've been instinctively taught to survive. Maybe we should take a lesson. We are all born with the inkling that there is something greater than ourselves that keeps us going to survive, and when we work together, we help each other arrive at that destination that will be best for all of us. Maybe it's time to listen to the voice inside our hearts and follow his leading. No more self-serving or tearing each other down. We are stronger as a body when we work together, passing the faith along to our brothers.

I looked down at my hands yesterday and was a bit startled at what I saw. Those hands didn't look like my hands. They looked like my mom's, and I have Dad's short stubby fingers that look just like his mother's. Have you ever taken a good look at your hands?

Think of all that you have accomplished with those hands. Maybe you've tenderly touched the face of a newborn or held the hand of someone in a retirement care center, cooked food for funerals and kids at school, held a stethoscope over someone's heart, or searched for a pulse in someone's wrist. You have arranged a funeral casket spray or made a delightful birthday bouquet or have used your index finger to guide young readers through the new reading book of the week. Maybe you've played a tune or lovingly stitched a quilt or wrote a story or a thank you note. The list is endless and could fill pages when you think about the history of your hands. Maybe your hands are smooth as silk with not a wrinkle in sight, or maybe your hands are red and rough from the work you do. Your hands are beautiful no matter what they look like, and they look the best when you are doing the work of your Maker. He gave us hands to use to help with the work of his kingdom, not to hurt others. Think about your hands today and do something good for him. You truly have the power to touch the world with your hands.

The word "compromise" has been swirling around in my brain for several weeks now. Not sure why other than it got stuck in the cobwebs, and I haven't been able to set it free. The word compromise has good and bad connotations. A good compromise is when two people who can't agree on something, both lay down their swords and agree to work together for the common good, putting their own wishes behind them for the benefit of others and agreeing to work together. The other side of compromise we have all seen, whether we want to admit it or not, the business proposal under the table that nobody sees, the adjusted figures on an income tax form, the roving eyes that saw the answer on someone else's test. I'll stop there. Each of us has to decide whether we stand on what we believe. Our integrity is who we are. Dependable, loyal, honest, and fair, no matter what? You do the right thing when being a bit shady would be to your benefit.

I have a feeling in the end if you caved, there would eventually be a wagon full of guilt to deal with. Regrets seek us out, and that's where we learn to ask for forgiveness and then deal with forgiving ourselves. No matter what you've done, or how far away from doing right you have gotten, there is one that offers a clean slate as far as the east is from the west. You will never need to compromise when you take a stand for him. If you haven't taken time to glance at the cross, take a minute and do so. When the words liar, cheater, and hater should be thrown at you for the awful things you've done, look at his shoulders. He has taken your blame so you don't have to.

*T*here is one lesson my parents taught me that has served me well. In fact, it may be engraved on the backs of my eyelids. "Thou shalt arrive early at all appointments, parties, services."

You get the picture. You will not arrive five minutes early. You will arrive at least fifteen minutes early, for if you arrive right on time, then you are late, and they wouldn't hear of arriving at "sixish" or "noonish" and sliding into whatever festivity five minutes late was totally unacceptable. Fashionably late was unheard of in their books. Have you ever prayed about something and begun to wonder if your prayers were getting through the roof of the house, let alone touching your Maker's ears? As they say, been there done that, and along the way, I have learned another lesson. When you pray about something specific, you need to believe that our God hears you. That's where faith kicks into gear, and once you feel assured that you have been heard, start thanking him for taking care of your request.

Our time frame and his don't always line up, thank goodness. Lazarus' family had given up. Imagine being dead four days, and then your family asks Jesus to bring you back, and you walk out of the grave? I have to wonder if he hated to come back as badly as Jesus probably didn't want to bring him back. Yet for his dear friends, he obliged and granted their request. Do not be discouraged. If you have sent up a request, and nothing appears to be happening, hold on to the railing of the boat that is being tossed on the waves of your storm. He hears and listens and answers on his time line, and after the storm is over, you will look back at the big picture and see that his timing is always perfect. It may not be the way you imagined, but he will come through for you. Always on time.

*L*ast night, I picked up our paper calendar to check and see which bills are due to be paid. Yes, I still write appointments and other reminders down as a way to help me remember. I enjoy having the written word in front of my face. It is the end of May already.

Didn't I just open this calendar to January? My goodness. The old saying that time flies when you are having fun must be true. And then I stopped and considered the miles I've traveled already this year and all the things we've done. Yes, we've been busy, and we hope it counts for him. Spending time with family, making new friends, offering hugs and smiles and shoulders to cry on, and just lending a helping hand. Then I open the newspaper to the page that remembers those who have gone on before us, and it reminds me that you never know when your days are going to be done. So today, I will do more than just go through the motions. I will help a neighbor or walk into my job with a smile on my face because I'm really working for my Maker. My employer just doesn't realize it. I will savor a moment of conversation with my spouse.

The spring flowers are blooming like crazy, and their scent makes my nose tingle. Living with intentions to honor him, not just filling another page in the book of life, making the days count, not merely racing to the final ending.

"They will be like a tree planted by the water that sends out its roots by the stream. It does not fear when heat comes. Its leaves are always green. It has no worries in a year of drought and never fails to bear fruit."

It is no secret that our family loves trees. The big, old stately trees that are hundreds of years old. You can't quite classify us as "tree huggers," yet we value beautiful trees. There are all kinds of trees around our home. Fruit trees, maple trees, oaks, and a couple of huge old sycamore trees just north of our property line. We value them for their shade, for holding the dirt in place, for providing some seasonal fruit, and for housing for the birds in the summer. They require sunshine and water to make them grow. They don't fret about anything, and they go about their business without bothering anyone. Minus the tossed limb during a storm once in a while. Yet when times get tough, and they don't have enough water. Their root system supplies their thirst.

When the noonday sun beats down upon them, they continue to stand tall. They don't shrink away and hide. A good lesson for all of us. Staying rooted in our Maker's words, depending only on him in the good times and bad. No matter what life throws at us, we are going to be alright. He will supply all our needs. We merely need to work like our needs depend on us and pray like it depends on him. A partnership that is the best.

There is a row in the hobby shops that I always have to peruse before I leave the store. The jigsaw puzzle aisle still intrigues me. I can look at the boxes of delightful pictures and be transported back many years to when my mom was still with us.

One of her winter traditions was to start a new jigsaw puzzle after the Christmas tree and decorations were stored away. After Christmas, if we happened to make a trip to the dime store, she would check out the puzzles that were on sale and bring a couple of them home. Then they were stored away until just the right time. There was quite a process involved getting the living room set up for the placing of the puzzle. The old pea green card table (that looked like heavy duty cardboard) was brought out of the entryway closet and set up in just the right spot in front of the picture window that afforded us optimum light. Next, she would decide which puzzle was the challenge for the winter and bring the box into the living room. She would gently hold the box, looking at all the pictures of the completed puzzle as if to memorize exactly how the picture was to look when finished. Then she poured the pieces onto the table. No hasty dumping of contents here lest a piece end up on the carpet. The box was put back together and taken to the closet and was never to be seen again, unless we got severely stumped putting the puzzle together and had to have help. At this time, we could now turn the puzzle pieces over to display their tops. After that was done, we all began the arduous task of finding the pieces for the frame of the puzzle. This went on for days, and whenever we had company, a few assorted friends and aunts, I was always baffled that they could walk over to the table and find that one piece that I had searched for and never was able to see and pop it into just the right spot.

The process of building this puzzle generally took weeks, depending on outside obligations, and it was always a sad day when the puzzle was finished and time to be taken apart and stored once again. If you poured all the pieces of your life onto a table, would you be able to put them back together again? Would some of the rounded corners be about worn off along with the images? Maybe you've had to put the same pieces back together one too many times, like trying to put a round peg in a square hole? Some of the pieces just don't fit together quite right, until you ask for help. Your Maker knows exactly how the puzzle of your life is supposed to look, and he waits to help you put the pieces together for your benefit. Try and try as you may to get the pieces snapped together just right, sometimes our best efforts just aren't enough, and we need some divine intervention to put it all together. He is the best at unscrambling tangled circumstances. No need to stay frustrated and puzzled. Help is just a prayer away.

*B*elieve it or not, some days, I just don't have words. No lightning-flash revelations or great life ponderables. So for the moment, I will be a little more quiet. I will take some time to reflect on the abundance of blessings that pour my way on a daily basis. I will continue to love friends and family with my prayers and remember that one of the best places to be is truly in someone's heart and prayers, telling my Maker how thankful I am to have each and every one in my life. I will consider those who have sacrificed their own lives to care for others, pastors, nurses, missionaries, delivery people, law enforcement and first responder folks, little people with eye problems along with other health problems, and some special older folks that inspire me with their keep going attitudes. Today my prayers will be a bit more specific and intentional. Praise God from whom all blessings flow.

The word "comfortable" just makes me feel good. Comfortable mattresses, easy sitting chairs, shoes that fit just right. Once in a while, if I get extremely tired, I have a tendency to feel cold, so I have a pair of pink pajamas that look like a long underwear top and pants that I put on. And the minute they are on me, I begin to warm up. Their softness is like wrapping myself in a hug. I usually don't wear them very long, just long enough to warm up and feel comfortable again. Some time ago, there was a commercial for some kind of laundry softener, and the advertisement showed a woman bringing a sheet off a clothesline into the house, and she popped the sheet up into the air, and the sheet floated down onto the mattress. I just know that whoever slept there had a comfortable night's sleep.

When I think of that sheet floating downward toward the mattress, I think of God's love, floating down on us. There truly is no better place to be when you feel alone, scared, or worried than under the canopy of his love, his comfort sent to us. Struggling today? Sit for just a moment at his feet read his word and let his umbrella of love cover you. The most comfortable place to be is close to him.

*A*s we started our drive through the canyon along the river this morning, we could see the water moving swiftly, and the snowmelt still had the water looking very murky, but that wasn't going to stop a crowd of adventurers from getting ready to hop into the river with both feet into the many rafts lined along the shore. People of all ages were wearing wet suits, with brightly colored life vests and white helmets. They looked like Lego people all lined up receiving instruction as to what was going to happen next. I love to watch the rafts coming down the river, the occupants mostly wearing smiles, and there is some evident excitement if they happened to catch some of the bigger currents. Love their zest for life, jumping into a challenge with both feet, giving it all they've got and working together to send their raft through some pretty rough water. Wouldn't it be nice if we could all hold on to our zest for life, to jump into living with both feet, all working together to weather the rough spots, and celebrating when we make it through on the other side? For some reason, though, we have a tendency to let life get us down, to carry the weight of the world on our shoulders. God is still God, and whatever our worries and problems, he can handle them. Maybe it's time for us to recover a bit of joy and try smiling again. In the end, if we belong to him, everything is going to turn out just fine. Find a sparkler this weekend, or a smoke bomb, or a black carbon snake that needs a spark set under him and try smiling, we have much to be thankful for! Time to jump into life.

That age-old questions of why do bad things happen to good people and the wicked prosper set up shop in my brain again this week. I've searched and searched for a positive, this is it answer to no avail. I've read other's theories, yet none satisfies me with a solid answer. Makes me think that, just maybe, I'm asking the wrong question. Since I can find no suitable answer, it is a waste of my time trying to find an answer, so once again I'm moving on. Instead, when I see a fellow traveler navigating a storm, I need to get busy and forget about the "why and wherefores." I should be asking what can I do to make this journey a little easier. Prayer is the first umbrella to go up. And then I can be a shoulder to cry on. Someone to lean on when my traveler gets weary. A hand to hold by just being available. In this day and age of quick media, I can call or text a "I'm thinking of you," a quick card of encouragement to be mailed.

I remember when I was navigating some stormy seas how much others checking on me meant. I need to do likewise. There are more pictures of flowers to be text and more I'm thinking of you messages to be sent. Let us never grow weary of doing good, being thankful that we are able to help, asking him to place us right where we need to be and to guide us every day.

*T*here are days that I start out with the best of intentions, going to spend a bit longer on my daily devotions and prayer time, eat better, exercise more, think only of good thoughts, and so on. And somewhere about early afternoon, I realize I have run completely off the rails, and the rest of the day soon becomes a wash. It's almost as if I am two separate people in opposing corners of a boxing ring. How did I get so off course? My plans were good. Maybe not solid, but honorable. Maybe I should've shored my intentions up a bit more. Got myself in order before I went to bed last night? All this brings my focus back to intentional living and allowing the Lord to order my steps, being flexible to his plans. Today I will resolve to do better, not just plan on it. My prayer list is long, and I need his reassurance from my owner's manual. Spending time in his presence is never a waste of time.

I love reading about the miracles Jesus performed. I marvel at his power and ability to take a hopeless situation and turn it into a victory for whomever is involved. The situations the doctors and scientists and people in the know say can't be fixed, and he does right before their very eyes, and I strongly believe that he still does these miracles today.

Recently I was reading a story about Jesus healing the blind man, and my first question is always, how did this man know which direction the pool was that he was about to go to and wash his eyes after Jesus placed mud on both eyes? This writer puts this miracle under the microscope and examines it even a bit further. It is our understanding that the blind man was born that way. He had never seen the light of day and had no point of reference for anything or a "mind's eye" with which to imagine. All he knew was total darkness. Upon further investigation, this writer suggests that the blind man has eyeballs but none of the necessary parts to make them work, no hard wiring to the brain. I had never given that statement any thought. My understanding was Jesus fixed the nonworking eyes, and I wasn't there when this miracle took place, so my theory may have been conjecture, maybe not. His theory does take this miracle to a whole new level. The blind man's obedience to wash his eyes was more than cleaning the mud away. When he washed, after Jesus touched his eyes, all of a sudden the nerves and tiny ligaments that weren't there when he was born suddenly appeared and started to function. Certainly something to think about. Whether the necessary parts of the blind man's eyes were installed and just not functioning or completely nonexistent really doesn't matter. He received his sight via the touch of his Maker. We all have situations that seem hopeless at times, and we are convinced that nothing can be done to correct those circumstances.

Try handing those situations to your Maker. He will make a way when there seems to be no answer. And maybe like the blind man, you will see the missing parts come into view, and the answers to your problems will be right before your eyes.

*S*tanding at the kitchen window of her little sod hut, the old woman sees dust up the roadway, which can only mean one thing—company is coming. She sees her husband walking faster than she's seen him walk in years as he goes to meet them. She doesn't recognize the three men. Evidently though, one of them must be someone important as she sees their servant boy head quickly to the cattle pen. Wonder what's up? Her husband sticks his head in the door and asks her to bake some bread. Preparations are soon in order, and beef sandwiches with all the trimmings an old woman can quickly put together are ready, and the men sat down to eat. The woman goes about putting her kitchen back in order half listening to the conversation from outside as it drifts through the window. She hears one say that she and her husband will conceive, and they will have a son. She chortles a giggle and the one who appears to be carrying the conversation comes to the kitchen and asks her if she laughed to which she replied no, as the color rises from the bottom of her neck to the tips of her ears.

The humor in this statement is just too much to handle. Both she and her husband are old, well past the age of having children. Nine months later, she gives birth to a son.

Never underestimate the providence and power of our Maker. Where there seems to be no answer, no solution to the problems we face or maybe have forgotten about, he has answers, and sometimes they come as the nicest surprises. Nothing surprises him, and he delights in you. Let your prayers be heard. He is waiting to answer them, in his time.

*H*ide and seek. Just the thought of that childhood game sends tingles down my back. I remember hiding under a desk where I was pretty well out of sight, and when I heard the finder's steps, the tingles became more intense, and I would forget to breathe. And if I remembered to shut my eyes, I wouldn't be found quite so quickly. I can hear the squeals and giggles now. Such fun!

I ran across a favorite scripture yesterday. "You will call my name. You will come to me and pray to me, and I will listen to you. You will search for me, and when you search for me with all your heart, you will find me."

For some reason, I always stopped reading at that point, but the next line grabbed me yesterday when I read it. "I will let you find me."

I'm not sure what that sentence says to you, but it ran right into my heart yesterday, when I need him. He isn't hiding. He is right there on my radar screen. I only need to look for him. He doesn't play games with us. He is always available. Maybe you've been hiding from him too long. Take a glance and find him right where he has always been, waiting for you to find him. His help is the best. Come just as you are. He will let you find him.

 $\mathcal{T}$ here is a kind of happiness that I think we forget about these days. So many problems in the world, loved ones and friends with severe illnesses, travel concerns, famine, travel safety, and the list is ever increasing. Some days, the load I carry on my back seems to get overwhelmingly heavy. Yesterday, about midmorning, I had this mind-boggling happiness begin to bubble up in my soul. What was the difference in yesterday and the many days before the "care quotient" become so large? I came to the conclusion that I'm a bit like a computer, only a little shorter in the memory department. Every once in a while, I need to run the scanner and clean my hard drive, discs, and anything else that begins to slow me down and steal my joy.

This has been a week, when I've seen prayer answered, not unlike any other week, and some of the concerns I've been asked to pray about have been monumental from small children to the elderly. So why did such joy build up inside yesterday?

Evidently I realized that I had done all I could do about each concern and handed them over to my Maker who is able to work mightily. For a day, I chose not to have a care in the world and to just be happy. The glow from inside my heart looked like ET on steroids. A most pleasant reminder that if we will let him handle our concerns, he will carry the load. No need to bog down and lose our happiness. He is still in control, and we merely need to prayerfully remember that his ways are so much higher than ours, and he can handle any prayer requests we give him.

$\mathcal{W}$e took a ride this morning to one of our favorite mountain overlooks. The altitude is high, and we can see way down the mountain to the valley below where a river runs. Tall pine trees cover the mountain sides, and we see pelicans floating through the air. Just an exquisite place to be. We have also been told by people who supposedly know that we wouldn't see any wildlife in the area. So we are cautious. Bear spray in the back pocket if we get out of the truck. This morning, when I stepped out of the truck and I put my foot on the dusty ground, my foot landed right next to a bear track. A very present reminder to be careful, even though those who know told us not to be concerned. We started back home and decided to stop and do a quick walk around the old airport that has nice walking trails and adjoins more forest area. We headed down the trail, and a pickup pulled up beside us, and a woman said to be careful if you go back into the forest as a grizzly was seen there yesterday. Another warning. We heeded her advice and walked the other direction toward the truck. There are warnings all around us, and common sense tells us to pay attention. Sometimes those who apparently are knowledgeable aren't always one hundred percent correct, in all walks of life. The old adage that says if it sounds too good to be true, it probably is reminds me of a surgeon in a well-known large hospital that did operations on a regular basis.

Someone got to snooping into his credentials and come to find out the supposed surgeon was a drug company representative but was practicing his surgical skill. A brother put some fur on his arms once pretending to be his brother. You never can tell. Trust your instincts. Heed the warnings, you receive as you travel along life's roadways, and if you have some doubts, check out your owner's manual, your Bible, and practice a little discernment. He will never lead you astray.

"Therefore, my dear brothers and sisters, stand firm. Let nothing move you. Always give yourselves fully to the work of the Lord, because you know that your labor in the Lord is not in vain."

The winds of change are blowing at our house, and I wondered last fall if we would survive just the thought, but thankfully we have survived, and retirement now looms ahead for both of us. We are a bit apprehensive, nervously excited and praying for many years of good health to enjoy this time together. We are so looking forward to seeing our kids who live away a little more often. Then there are some hunting trips in the works and just some plans to drink coffee on the deck and watch the sunrise together, for a change. No more race out the door to the work truck when the phone rings and storms. We will ride them out just like the rest of the world. Not having a cement schedule is very inviting and a little intimidating too; however, don't expect to see us sitting in rocking chairs, at least for very long. Our earthly employment is coming to an end, yet we have things to do for him, and we are anxious to get busy for him, wherever we are or go. This is going to be the dessert on top of the full plates we've had for many years. We prefer wearing out to rusting out, and after all we've been blessed with and what he did for us, how can we do any less? Time for change, so we best get busy.

*Y*esterday, as I watched the birding activity from the deck, I got quite a chuckle watching the blue jays, one in particular, trying to peck loose the sunflower seed on the big frozen suet cake that sits in a clay pottery dish on the deck rail. I honestly thought he might be brain-dead by the time he finished hammering away at the frozen seed. Right there next to him, in a shallow metal dish, was fresh sunflower seed not frozen down. Every once in a while, he would stop pecking at the frozen suet cake and go over to the loose seed, grab a bite, and come back to the cake and hammer some more. Seems he wanted what he couldn't have more than what was within reach that he didn't have to struggle for. I shouldn't have chuckled.

Fast forward a couple of hours, and I decided to take the new coffee maker apart and clean it. I took the little filter basket that swings off its post and cleaned it well, shined it right up, and then tried to reinstall it. For at least fifteen minutes, I struggled trying to get this little basket put back on the post after I cleaned it so it would close. I had the coffee maker laying on its side and even got out the screw driver for some less than gentle persuasion to no avail. In total frustration, I took off my work gloves, set the coffee maker right side up, and tried one more time, and bingo, when I pushed the little basket upward onto its post, it slid right in. A quick peek outside and once again, a goldfinch was captured inside the pickle jar squirrel feeder and couldn't find his way out of the jar. Sunflower husks were flying at tornadic speed as he beat his wings looking at the bottom of the jar trying to get out. My thought was just turn around and look toward the light. The hole you flew into the jar through is ten times bigger than you, and you can fly back out. The minute I removed the jar from its stand, out the bird flew. We are a comical bunch, with or without feathers. The yearning for something out of reach when we have everything we need at our finger tips.

There was a booklet that came with the coffee maker, and it had the instructions to clean the filter basket written in my language, and my job would've been much easier had I taken the time to consult the instructions. The bird in the bottom of the squirrel feeder jar just needed to back out of the corner the same way he flew in. We don't have to struggle so hard.

If your frustration level is a bit high with the life you live today, help is as close as the mention of your Maker's name. He also has an instruction manual, our Bibles, that addresses every corner you get backed into. Life is so much easier when we follow his lead, being contented with what he provides for us. So much easier than trying to do life on our own our way. His ways are tried and true. Simply the best.

Just when I think there are no more possible home remodeling television shows, they change venues to a different town, and we're off to the races again. The words "ship lap and subway tile" are every day terms, walls are torn-down, and cabinets get a face lift. It is amazing to me that the contractors and crews are able to take an older home that needs some love, and these folks totally transform the weary, worn houses into a fresh, clean, new-looking dwelling place. All the old blemishes are gone. Kind of like when we realize that we need our Maker's presence in our lives and a fresh coat of paint. We need a sturdy foundation, one without cracks that is solid to stand the test of time. We need adequate infrastructure to support us. His blueprints for us to build on. Locks to keep the bad stuff away and at bay. And we need to remember routine maintenance to repair the splotches and cracks that show up. He will do his part if we will just remember to do our part. New creations repaired by his love. He does the best at fixing us up. No better remodel exists.

*H*is master replied, "Well done, good and faithful servant! You have been faithful with a few things. I will put you in charge of many things. Come and share your master's happiness!"

These days, life is a bit like a marathon, or maybe a sprint. If you aren't able to participate in the race any more, you can certainly encourage from the sidelines by shouting encouraging words, or maybe you can quench someone's thirst with a cool drink. And if you are still able, lend a shoulder and hold someone up as they cross the finish line. Finishing the race together, helping each other along well done, good and faithful servant, will be music to my ears.

*J*ust for a moment, think of four of your favorite people, family members, coworkers, and neighbors, and every year you plan a get together to share life's stories and reconnect.

Love one another and do activities together. Your time is limited, so you pack as much as you can into the time you share together. Imagine that you are making plans for the next reunion, and one of your beloved friends or family or whatever notifies you at the last minute and tells you that they are no longer coming. Everyone in the group is devastated. Each person is an integral part of the party, and it's just not going to be the same without them there. Everyone scratches their heads and tries to remember if something was said or done that might've offended the missing person, but to no avail. The person no longer coming gives no excuse, and any contact with the person is completely severed.

Everyone has very sad hearts and misses this person so very much, and nobody understands why they have pulled away. You know how very much you miss them. Do you suppose your Maker feels the same when you pull away and think you no longer need his presence in your life? He has created us and longs to be a part of our lives. Maybe you've never met Him. It's never too late to belong to him. He knew you and everything about you before you were a twinkle in someone's eye or knit together in your mother's womb. You are an integral part of his family, and he longs to reconnect or stay connected. There is nothing that can keep you away from him. Nothing that you have done is too terrible to come back to him. He offers mercy and grace and forgiveness. If you haven't been in contact with him for a while, give him some thought. His heart breaks when we turn away. We are part of the family of God, the best family to belong to.

I love hugs, those I'm so glad to see you with arms wrapped around you or a hug from the side. I received a hug several days ago that left me thinking. This hug was different. I walked away thinking. For that brief moment, I was all this person was thinking about when they hugged me. No quick come here hug but an in the moment-type hug. No racing off to carry on the activities of the day. We miss so many special moments in our day-to-day lives just because we are so preoccupied and busy. Maybe if we would slow down at least for a couple of minutes a day, the ordinary would again become extraordinary, and we might even see our Maker's hand in our surroundings. People are around us daily. Take a moment and let them know what they mean to you, or just say thanks for being there, but really "be" there. Stop your mind for just a moment. There is something really special about genuine emotion. Don't take that emotion for granted around the one you love. We all love to be acknowledged. "Thanks for being my friend." Now smile. You will feel so much better.

*H*ang around a three-year-old for a while, and you may just start to question everything you know, as a three-year-old wants to know the answer to "why" in detail, and "just because" doesn't cut it. Makes one's perspective begin to freshen with old "ponderables" becoming new again. One begins to rethink short concise answers that are easy to understand, especially when explaining that answer to a little one. A child's ability to take an answer, at face value, with all the faith they know, not jaded by the charades the world is throwing out, makes me smile and warms my heart. Your answer is all they need. No preconceived notions about ulterior motives or hidden meaning. Heaven knows, it is hard to trust anyone anymore as an adult. We read way too much baggage into everything. Step away from the world's noise for a while and remember simpler times when you were a child and life was a bit more simple and easier to understand. Dare to remember the times when people answered your questions and you gladly accepted those answers, and that was that, period. Don't understand all that is going on in our world and in your personal life? Open your Bible, and with a clear, quiet mind, begin to read. The stories and instructions contained within those pages are for you and me and our best interests. Come back to the God of your youth and be refreshed. There is a reason that we need to come to him as a child. Faith at its finest. No other answers needed.

"We're following the leader, the leader. We're following the leader wherever he may go." A delightful little song that I heard many, many times as our children were growing up, a song from a favorite movie. What makes a "good" leader? Let' see.

A leader needs to know where he's going. Where the dangerous parts of the journey are. He must be devoted to his task, more concerned about the welfare of the folks following him than his own safety. Someone who is called to lead. The one thing you don't want to hear a leader say, "This doesn't look familiar." Now what makes a "good" follower?

Someone who is willing to follow another's leadership. To stay in line and not try to get ahead of the leader. Who is considerate of those behind him. Who pays attentions to his surroundings and doesn't gawk around. Someone who also is alert to danger, who helps his fellow travelers along, and who knows his place and is devoted to it. Are you a leader or a follower? Personally, I like following, letting others make the big decisions, yet I'm very cognizant of their guidance which means I like to be sure that their leading is authentic, honest, true, and lines up closely with my own personal belief system. Leaders have a lot of responsibility and need to stay on their toes as we follow. If you have ascribed to the wrong leader off and on through life and find yourself lost in the fray, there is one whose leading is the best. He will never guide you off course. His only concern is your welfare. He knows where he is and where you are going. His timing is perfect. No need to try and get ahead of him. Following the best leader ever. A faithful dependable shepherd. One who would leave the ninety-nine to find you. Makes life a pleasure to follow, letting him lead.

*T*his past week has been one that leaves you scratching your head in wonderment about the people you interact with. We were walking our daily route, and this area is known for four wheelers and all things motorcycle. We try to stay out of their way and for the most part the driver's reciprocate. The trails we take are now dusty, so doing wheelies and donuts is the norm. The first four wheeler we encountered saw us walking and took the next trail over so as not to spray us with dust, and we truly respected his decision. Then there were two more four wheelers that approached us. The first buggy had what we are assuming was a father and son; the second most likely was his wife and daughter. They stopped about thirty feet from us, and then all of a sudden, he hit the pedal to the metal and came straight for us. I honestly thought we were going to have to jump into the trees. As he was enjoying his weaving in the dust, headed for us, we wondered about him and the dirt tornado he showered us with as well as his family in the buggy behind him. Quite a teaching moment for his son and family. Yet he wasn't the only one that left us wondering.

We stopped at a big box store to load up on supplies and groceries and waited in the checkout line for almost forty-five minutes. The store was swamped with people back to school shopping. Grocery shelves were empty, and only three cashiers were working when there were at least thirteen checkout aisles. And the self-checks were spilling over into the aisle too. Our cashier was wonderful and apologetic and thanked all of us many times for being patient, which was really refreshing as several feet over there was a lot of hollering going on, and I seriously was looking for a place to get down on the floor lest bedlam ensued. So why have I typed all of this? We learned a lesson this week. We could've been blistering mad by the crazy antics around us, but we decided that these situations weren't going to steal our joy no matter what, and that lesson has stuck. We each have the power to let life throw us a curve, yet when we choose to ignore all the little idiosyncrasies and let them slide off like water off a duck's back, we defuse the whole situation and come through with a bit of sanity and retain our joy. Joy is a choice, and each one of us has that choice often on a daily basis. From now on I am going to try to be more intentional and not grab the steering wheel so tightly, and maybe when someone pulls a stunt, I will be able to just smile and say God bless you. You do not have the power to take my joy, and I won't willingly let you. Today the grumbles are gone, and I will choose to be joyful. After all, I know where the joy comes from. Smile a little more today. You might just make everyone wonder what you're up to, choosing joy.

"Gee, I wish I'd known sooner." How many times have you heard that statement or maybe said it yourself? You find yourself feeling left out. Maybe you could have offered a friend or family member some support during a rough patch. You would do anything in your power to help if you could, but you just didn't know something was wrong or someone needed some help and support. There are times that we literally don't know what to do or say in a situation, yet when we show up and are available, support means so much, and words are often not necessary.

Last summer, a friend remarked that he needed to get back to God, and not knowing exactly where he stood at that point, I shared my faith journey. I wasn't eloquent. No fancy words. No lightening from the sky. Just my experience when I decided to commit to follow my Maker, and after I got through, I apologetically told him that I hoped he wasn't overwhelmed.

His reply is still engraved in my heart today. "I would rather you throw me a life ring before I drown than after."

So you have nothing to be ashamed of when you share your faith. And if you are prompted to do so, go ahead. You might just be the answer someone is looking for. Don't worry. Let him take the lead. Tiny little seeds that fall in the forest may lie dormant for years, and all of a sudden a raging wildfire consumes that seed, and after the fire is over, a little green shoot begins to emerge from the ground. Before you know it, that little shoot is a tree, tall and strong. Yet if the seed had never dropped to the ground, and the fire hadn't happened, it would just be a tiny dormant seed. He is sharing his love with a hurting world, dropping one tiny seed at a time, for his kingdom is loving always, first in word and then in deed.

"*T*he high cost of living." Do those words make you cringe? At least once a year, we are caught off guard by the increase of the costs of goods and services we use and the imbalance of our income. Yet when we look at what it cost us to live comfortably, we're not sure what we need or want to let go of. The cost of heating and cooling divided by the number of days you use it, the special brand of coffee we enjoy, the restaurants we eat at. What are we willing to give up to make our hard-earned dollars stretch a little farther? We love our creature comforts, and being comfortable is awfully nice. Yet am I willing to do without anything?

None of us like pain or being uncomfortable, yet we growl about what it costs us to be comfortable. Let's change thoughts for the moment. What about the high cost of loving? Are you able to give your all for someone else, spouse, friend, child, neighbor, stranger on the street, or your country? Putting someone else's needs and comfort above your own? How many extra miles are you willing to walk? How many extra coats are you willing to buy? How many meals are you willing to serve? A life of service for others. Then how about the high cost of dying? Are you willing to lay down your life for your fellow man as a patriot or as a witness to an injustice? What are you willing to give?

We have an extraordinary example of dying for others, and we find that in our creator's Son, knowing what was ahead of him yet willing to trudge up a hill with a heavy cross on his back for you and me. Maybe when we get tired of the high costs of living comfortably, of giving our all to the thankless, we should remember what giving a life looks like, and maybe just then we can find the kind of humility our creator requests. Everything we have comes from him. We owe him everything. Our living and loving and our willingness to die. No greater love was ever shown. Can we do any less?

*L*ast week as we were running errands, we decided to grab a bite to eat in a cozy little Mom and Pop's diner. It was very warm and welcoming, quite comfortable, with friendly wait staff, and the food was very good. There was a sign when you came into the diner that said to please wait to be seated, and the staff seated you quickly. We were about halfway through our meal, when a very tall, overly dressed, young man walked in wearing a heavy insulated coat and stocking cap. He strode past our booth and proceeded to seat him-self. As he passed by, it was apparent he hadn't been near a shower for quite some time, yet we just tried to ignore the odor. Within seconds our server headed down the back hall, and the manager returned with her, a small young woman, and she approached the man and asked him to come with her, which he did. Then they stopped right behind our booth. She reminded him that he was welcome in the diner, yet there were some stipulations that he hadn't followed, which clued us in that he had been there before. She very calmly and firmly reminded him that they had an agreement, and then we didn't hear much more of the conversation until the end. We were just a little bit nervous as the young man got a bit agitated and loud, and sadly, in this day and age, you had to wonder what might happen next? They finished their conversation, and I heard the manager tell the young man that he was welcome to come back after he had done whatever she required, and she would be happy to serve him herself and fix him a box of food to take with him.

This event may not seem out of the ordinary, but we saw some-thing that made us smile—compassion. The young manager was so kind yet firm. She never talked down to him, and by the time the young man left, all appeared to be well. I wonder how often we try to race ahead in this life, when we need to be holding to the path he has prescribed for us and his instructions. We bump into a roadblock or a wall and wonder why? Living a life for him, trusting him with his perfect timing, allowing ourselves to wait on Him, and then being able to fly through whatever situation, sharing his love and compassion as we go through our days. The best days ever happen with him at the helm.

*F*or just a minute, grab a cup of coffee and take a seat at the dining room table. Join me in perusing a magnificent cooking magazine and turn to page thirty-six. Look at that cake! The glossy magazine page makes this cake unbelievably beautiful, triple layer, double chocolate, with dark chocolate butter cream icing and a touch of smooth decadent decoration. Let's say chocolate curls. We decide we are going to make the cake, so we write down a list of ingredients, and off to the store we go. We are able to buy almost everything the recipe calls for, yet we have to make some substitutions because some of these special ingredients are unavailable in our area. With great fervor, we come home and bake the cake using the necessary substitutions. The cake turns out good yet doesn't really look like the beautiful specimen pictured on the magazine page, and the taste?

Well, it's just so so. We lament the fact that the grocery store just didn't have those special ingredients readily available for purchase, so our cake just isn't what we expected. The picture, or the vision, of the cake was stunning, yet when we finished our cake, the resemblance was similar yet not the same. So if your friends put you under the looking glass, what will they see? Are you a beautiful specimen of a human that is on the run all the time, calling from folks who need you go unanswered to voicemail on your phone only to be discovered at the end of the day past everyone's bedtime? Are you consumed with busyness, or are you a human that is available? Your friends know that when they need to talk or ask for help. You are ready, and, Johnny, on the spot, you will help in seconds flat.

Drop everything else and take the call. No voicemail for you. Sometimes we have great visions and ideas about what we should be doing, yet we are called by our Maker to be available first. Everything else will fall into place. Those who need us don't need our high expectations and visions. They need our availability, and if you can't find anyone who fills the bill, your Maker is always available. He won't block your calls. Your calls won't go to voicemail. He is always available and just waits for you to ask for his help, and for that I am thankful always. There will never be any substitutions for his love. He is the real deal, and there is always a direct line to him. It's your call.

*D*o you give one hundred percent of yourself to everything you do? Relationships, family, employment, volunteer activities? What holds you back or keeps you from it? Fear, not enough confidence, not qualified, just want to keep a little of yourself in reserve lest things turn sour and you need an escape clause?

My favorite author has recently written a book about loving with abandon at all times. This stretches the elastic on my imagination. There are people I really don't care for, for a variety of reasons, yet maybe it's not the people, it's their beliefs. The Bible reminds me that I'm to love my neighbor as myself, and there is no "if" in that sentence. If they share my beliefs, if they go to the same church I do, if they live life similar to mine. Makes me wonder why we feel the need to add qualifications to his word. You may surprise people when you act like you truly like them no matter what, putting others above yourself, and they may just tell you they've never met anyone quite like you, and then you can smile because you know why. Sharing his love above all else across political, religious, and business lines. It seems to me that he didn't hold back on my account. Maybe I shouldn't hold back either. Loving always first.

*A*s a child, I never went to many carnivals. Maybe once or twice. My dad worked hard and wasn't about to toss coins at what he deemed useless entertainment. Yet I remember how enticing some of the game booths were with brightly colored lights and balloons and the coolest stuffed animals you had ever seen. All kinds of noisy and daring rides and food that you could only get at the carnival. To a young child, this was an exciting place to be.

Somewhere along the line, though, I was the recipient of a big red and white teddy bear, and I adored that bear. However, not long after I got to bring him home, a little thread began to unravel at the seam where he was sewn together, and tiny little balls of Styrofoam stuffing began their escape. It wasn't long before the bear started to become limp, and I realized it hadn't been made very well but rather made cheaply and just wasn't what I expected it to be, not a very high-quality bear. Sometimes we invest ourselves in our own wants and desires, just to find out that isn't what we really wanted. Relationships that go sour. Homes and stuff that we become slaves to. Jobs that seem like dream jobs that are not on the up and up. And we wonder why we ever thought we wanted what we have received? If you are looking for authenticity and work that is real, maybe it's time to consider visiting with your Maker. He is the real deal and won't let you down. Ask him to use you. Making a living for the family is necessary, but if you want to do more, ask him to use you at your work. Opportunity will come. Ask Him for wisdom and consult his word when you have decisions to make. See if all your wants and wishes line up with him first. Remembering to keep a servant's heart, helping make our world a little kinder one good deed at a time. All of us have a tiny empty spot in our hearts, yet when filled with his love, whatever we do in his name is so much more gratifying and satisfying. The best way to start a new week, or a new day, is with him in the pilot's seat.

*T*his week, it seems everyone has needed an extra dose of "hope." Thinking about what makes people resilient intrigues me. Diet, exercise, books, they read optimism. What kind of fuel do these folks use to fan their flames and keep them going? In search of some answers, I was drawn to the book of 1 Thessalonians the first chapter, and I think I may have found some answers. These folks had been taught well, and they stayed strong in their faith no matter what came their way. They were energetic about serving the Lord. They waited expectantly for his return, yet they didn't just sit and wait. They were busy, and their energetic passion spilled over to others. They were well grounded and established. They lived with the faith and assurance that no matter what happened, they would be fine because they belonged to him and served him in every capacity that was available to them.

When they received God's word, they stood on it. No wavering. And they were enthusiastic. No ho hum hum drums. Almost makes me want to clean the sink with a toothbrush. Well, maybe life bogs us down, and we forget that he is still in control. So maybe living energetically, no matter how old you are, being established and growing in your relationship with him daily, being open and willing to learn, and then showing a bit of enthusiasm. People who are excited about what they are doing are contagious, and we enjoy their company. Today, maybe it's time to pull up our suspenders, hop into the tennis shoes and get busy, and maybe smile a little more. Thankful for teachers of the faith that remind us to lose the "Eeyore" syndrome and live with a little more joy, every day.

"My hope is built on nothing less than Jesus Christ, my righteousness. All other ground is sinking sand."

Random thoughts pop into my head, and last evening as I was winding down getting ready for bed, I just happened to remember as a young girl that my mom deemed it necessary for me to have a "hope" chest. The chest itself was a cardboard box, nothing fancy. And as I worked through high school, occasionally I would purchase a slotted spoon or a special spatula or a gizmo that I thought would be handy when setting up a new home. Mom would surprise me once in a while with a utensil to add to my larder from money saved back for the egg delivery route that afforded her purchase. Occasionally I would take inventory of my hope box and see what was really necessary that I didn't have. So I had a goal for the next time I had a few extra coins. My hope chest served me well, and many of the goodies it contained have been used until they had to be replaced. Many years later, I was headed down the road with a cancer diagnosis, and my hope was a bit shaky, until one day when a friend said to me, "You will be fine no matter what the outcome is."

My hope bounced back, and I clung to those words several times especially when the water threatened to take me under. You can place your hope in the weather report or your bank statement or the newest trend you choose to follow. Yet if you are looking for something solid, there is one who is much more reliable. His love isn't affected by the weather report or your latest stock statement or the latest fad swirling around. He is rock solid, and if you're looking for hope to cling to, look no further. He is the solid rock. Everything else is sinking sand.

*H*ave you been or maybe you are in a dark season of life, where the long gray hallway is too long, and you can't quite see the light at the end of the tunnel? We've all been there, and we ponder what the outcome is going to be.

I read a story yesterday that gives a bit of perspective, and it isn't my story but rather another's. A young man in high school lost his eyesight, and being the brave courageous soul that he was, he decided that he was going to master the high jump. So he enlisted a friend to be his eyes. His friend started walking ahead of this young man on the track and calling to him so that the blind man would get used to his voice and learn to follow it. Not long after this training session, the young man decided he was ready for the high jump. So they started training for the event. The blind man learned how many steps to run before he jumped and listened to his friend's voice at all times, and he jumped and did amazingly well. Then came the day that he was signed up for a challenged athlete's contest. With an arena of parents and loved ones looking on, the young site-challenged boy had three attempts. The first attempt he did great, but on the second attempt, his friend's voice got distorted, and when the jumper jumped, he did a face plant in the cement. Medical personnel rushed to check him out, and he was scraped up but ready for one more try. The third attempt, and he nailed it. There is a lesson in this for all of us. As long as we keep listening and looking for our Maker, we will survive the long gray tunnels of life. His light is right there. We just need to keep looking for it, and maybe we can't quite see where he is. We need to be straining to listen for his voice. He calls us daily, and he loves us so much. Even when we don't understand the circumstances we find ourselves drowning in, he is beside us, until the end of the age. He is "with" us, comfort like no other. We may face plant off course, but he will welcome us back, always, and set our feet back on the path he has chosen for us.

"There is no greater love." There's that word "love" again. Sentimental cards with beautiful verses and prose gorgeous red roses wrapped in tissue paper and ribbons. The finest chocolates. A piece of unique jewelry. Or sitting in a hospital room holding the hand of someone you "love" who isn't doing so well. Rocking a baby in the wee early hours of the morning because you "love" that baby and would do anything to soothe a nasty tummy ache. Making sure a neighbor that is struggling has a warm meal. Looks to me like the word "love" is much more a "doing" word than the sentiments of the finest Valentine's card. And both are equally nice. There is a kind of "love" that I'm not sure we all understand so well though. The kind of "love" that says I will step in between the gunman and my coworker. The kind of "love" that protects the borders of our country so we can sleep in peace at night. The kind of extravagant "love" that says that these are my people and I will take their punishment so that they don't have to. I'm not a big fan of punishment or discipline for that matter. And to say that I would take responsibility for an act that was wrong that someone else committed so they wouldn't have to be served punishment is beyond my borders. A little farther out of the box than I care to imagine if I'm painfully honest. Yet someone who loves us so much did exactly that many years ago for our benefit, because he "loves" us that much. Wow. The next time you ponder the word "love," stretch just a bit further. Put the running shoes on and hop into action. Making loving a "doing" word in your world. The best way to show our mixed up world who he is. Loving first without an agenda or strategy. Showing difficult people that we don't' need to spread anger and judgment. Just putting "love" into action. He is the greatest example, and I'm thankful every day for his love.

*H*onesty, what a beautiful attribute. I remember when honest people were held in high esteem and employers scrambled to hire such a person. Now finding a person who is honest can lead to quite a search. Why is that? Every so often I hear the comment that your truth is not the same as mine. And that leaves me scratching my head. You are either honest or not. As a society, we have become so accepting, and we try not to offend one another, but the truth still matters. Don't look to social or mainstream media for the truth. Sadly it doesn't often exist in either situation. So where do we look to find the truth? Let's refresh our memories. "I am the way, the truth, and the life." So it looks like to find honesty and the truth, we start at square one in our owner's manual, our Bibles. The great I am is the truth, and he accepts no substitutes to make us comfortable or allow us to feel accepted. As we start a new day or week, maybe it would be a good idea to do a bit of self-check and see where our honesty and truthfulness stand. We may think we've hidden our dishonesty from him and others, but sadly, the truth always wins in the end. Time to start with a clean slate? Checking the conditions of our hearts and minds, because he won't settle for less. He's always waiting for us to come clean, and he loves us in spite of ourselves and our misspoken words. The best friend ever, always, lovingly honest.

*Y*esterday, it was declared that someone's archery bow needed some tweaking at the local shop, and while we were at it, we would do some chores and pick up some groceries. Today we hopped into our most comfortable clean tee shirts and jeans and headed up the road not giving much thought to our shirts. We were almost to town when the driver looked over at me and said, "You seriously had to dress like me?"

We both laughed and headed on.

At lunchtime, we stopped at a favorite place for a quick bite, and as we were sitting there, we started noticing the T-shirts others were wearing. Most of the shirts declared a place the wearer had just visited. Sort of like a badge of honor that said look where I've been. Then I looked down at my shirt, and my throat clamped shut. On my shirt was a small cross, and I thought, *Yes, I've visited that cross many times and will continue to do so as long as I'm alive.*

The beautiful place where I lay my burdens down, where I found the promise of eternal life, where I find forgiveness for all my sins. A beautiful reminder that we need to remember where we came from and who we represent. Revisiting back at the beginning where my roots began to grow, still seeking him every day.

*E*ncouragement, a word that invokes hope. A portion of scripture I read this past week dealt with a group of new believers, and their teachers that had been with them for some time and were called away for a while, yet this group was always in the prayers of their teachers. These new believers faced some trials and persecution, yet they held tight to their faith never wavering. And when one of the teachers returned to check on these folks, he was the one that was encouraged because of their faith. They were serving one another with compassion and loving each other through the various trials. I think these folks were truly onto something good. It really doesn't matter if you are a lifetime believer or someone new to the faith, there are going to be some rough patches no matter how big your faith is. Hold fast to him, and he will help you ride out the storm. He's been known to tell the storm to stop and peace ensued. May your day be filled with strength and compassion not because of who you are but because of "whose" you are. Hold tight to your faith. He won't let you down. May you find his peace in your today and every day.

"Come to me, all who are weary and burdened, and I will give you rest." One of Webster's definitions of rest says rest is a bodily state characterized by minimal functional and metabolic activities. I remember seasons in my own life when "rest" seemed fleeting, and I was physically and mentally exhausted from work and responsibilities as a parent and as a child. Rest was nowhere to be found. Just keep pushing and going through the motions, the light is at the end of the tunnel. Days that ran one into another. I began to wonder how much more of me there was left to give, yet somehow, with his help and strength, I made it through. Now I can look back and say that I never regretted a moment of the "busyness." Incredible memories are etched in my heart and mind. Sometimes just a few moment of silence away from all the noise, sitting at his feet, is all it takes to refresh us, and we can carry on. Rest. Curling up in your favorite recliner nestled under your favorite fuzzy blanket. No noise from the world around us. Just a few moments of peace and quiet, and soon you are ready to face the world and all of your responsibilities again. He is our strength. He allows us to rest for our physical and mental health. Take time to grab a few moments and regroup. Your world won't stop, and you will be better able to carry on. I am so thankful for rest every day or any day that I can stop for just a few moments and sit with him.

*F*requently as we travel around the forests admiring the scenery, we see signs that say, "Please leave this camp site in better condition than you find it." Sadly, not everybody pays attention and leaves the site worse, but for the most part the sites are in good condition. That sign has become our own personal motto, not just for campsites though. For the people we interact with, the places we visit, the conversations and texts we take part in. What can we do individually and intentionally to make the world we live in a better place? A smile and a kind word to the server that dishes your meal, a pleasant greeting to the person behind the counter at the gasoline station, maybe even offering a word of encouragement. A special time of uninterrupted prayer for folks that are struggling. Allowing someone to step in line ahead of you in the cashier's line. It takes so little effort to be kind and considerate. Putting others first, serving them with his love, helping to make the weary roads we travel a little easier to navigate. We're all in this together. It's not about us. It's all about him always. May we always remember.

I looked at the top of my head where my hair is thinning and asked God to please put some hair back there, and then in my mind's eye, I saw the sweet face of a little girl battling cancer with all the life she has with not a hair on her head, and I felt terribly small. I complained about the uncomfortable shoes on my feet. Then I remembered the young man wearing flip flops made from empty Mountain Dew pop bottles that had been flattened and had twine running between his toes to keep them on his feet. And I looked at my feet and hung my head. We took a long walk, and I growled about my aching hips and tired knees, and then I remembered a young man who is working hard to stand up and walk from the confines of a wheelchair and would love to have tired legs from walking. A lump formed in my throat. My trifocals make it difficult to walk, and I think of a man who has never seen anything. I asked someone to repeat what they had just said and remembered the dear soul who could hear nothing at all. Dear God, please let me remember how blessed I am and appreciate all you have given me. Remind me not to complain, about anything. Forgive me for being so small when so many others would love to be in my shoes. Forgive me, Lord, I am eternally grateful for everything you have blessed me with. Help me remember it all comes from you. Amen.

There is a very special bookshelf in our office room. The shelves were made by a cousin many years ago and have withstood the test of time and weight of various treasures.

There is a set of very, very old encyclopedias bought at an auction, and those books belonged to a certain golf team's bus driver's parents, and, yes, just for him, we take one of those heavy old books down and read occasionally. The Internet is faster, but there is a special connection with an old book. There are also some quilting magazines or projects that stand waiting on "someday", and if I was generous, I won't live long enough to get these projects finished. Then there is a box of glass cutting supplies that have never been opened that I thought I needed. A few other "how-to" books that have never been read and on the list goes. Which brings me to the conclusion that I haven't learned anything from those stored books either. I could learn how to be a mechanic by reading one of those books, but until I actually raise the hood of a car and stand beside a skilled mechanic to learn how to fix whatever, my book has only been for information. I could watch a video to learn to crochet, but until I sit beside someone that is crochet savvy and learn by watching and doing, the video really hasn't done me much good. The same goes for my owner's manual, my Bible. I can read and memorize all the pages, yet if I don't do what that manual instructs me to do have I gained anything besides knowledge. Seems to me there needs to be a heart connection. Reading his word and putting those words into practice, the best advice ever, and you will find joy in those pages. The best guidance ever. Maybe it's time to open his book, read a chapter, and then get to work. And then thank him for what you learned, today, and every day of the week.

*F*or just a moment, imagine that you have a furry, four-footed canine that you adore.

When you arrive home from a long day's work, your fuzzy pet is so very happy that you are home. Do you ever wonder what that ball of fur would say to you if it could talk?

"How did your day go? Did you get a lot accomplished? Who did you see? Where did you go? I've been here waiting anxiously waiting for you to come home, and it feels like an eternity since I've seen you, yet I waited. I didn't go anywhere. Completely hypothetical questions. There is nothing quite like a furry faithful friend for unwavering companionship. Even when that pet isn't treated the best, it will still love you. As much as a pet is able to adore you, how much more do the people around you love you? Then there is your Maker. Maybe you've pushed him into the background as you've traveled life's road, took your own path, and followed your own whims. Didn't really feel a need for guidance from anyone, yet you are beginning to realize something is missing in your life. Life isn't as smooth as it's all cracked up to be. Your Maker is patient, and he hasn't gone anywhere and hasn't moved away, and he waits for you and me to ask him to be a part of our lives. He won't ask you about the details of your journey without him. He already knows but will welcome you with open arms, complete acceptance, and unfailing love. A love that is so big that he gave up his own Son for all the wrongs you and I have ever done. Maybe it's time to hand him the reigns. Let Him take the wheel and guide. I can guarantee that he will never steer you wrong. You and I were made to serve him. When you get tired of doing life your way, he waits for you to ask him to help. Always available and won't let you down. You can trust his heart. What are you waiting for?

*T*here is an early morning chill in the air. The aspens are beginning to change into their beautiful fall clothing, and many of the resident bushes have turned golden in the canyons. The season of change is upon us. After the oppressive heat and humidity and the record drought of the summer, the rain has started again and is refreshing the soil. Hopefully there will be a few crunchy apples and a pumpkin or two as we welcome fall. Whatever happens, he is in control, and we may never understand the hows or whys or the timing, but learning to trust is imperative. Change isn't always easy or pleasant, no matter the situation. As fall returns, have you grown some this summer? Have you peeled off layers of clothing to stay as comfortable as possible? Did you peel any unnecessary layers in your faith walk as well? Maybe losing some hurt feelings, anger, regrets, and letting go of situations that hinder your walk with him? As we prepare for a new weather season, it might be a good time to look at how we will be clothing ourselves. The deep rich fall colors, burgundy, gold, deep brown, and greens, an extra layer of protection to keep us warm on chilly days. Yet we don't need to worry about our clothing as long as we are clothed with his attributes, loving hearts, compassionate eyes, hands that reach out to lend a hand up, shoulders for other to lean on, and ears that always have time to listen, raising the bar on what we can do and what we are willing to do to serve others. The best designer clothing you will ever wear in any season.

"*A* man's heart plans his way, but the Lord directs his steps."

Monday night before I called it a day, I had my Tuesday plans in place and ready, just so I thought. I knew exactly how my day would go. I knew what I had to get done, and when my feet hit the floor on Tuesday morning, I was off and running. The first order of the day was to terminate a media subscription that we had used for many, many years. All I wanted to do was cancel my subscription. After visiting with multiple robots and six actual customer representatives, the company agreed to my request yet not without some begging on their part for us to remain loyal customers. I thought I was done. Mission accomplished. Equipment was taken to the proper drop off point, and no, neither carrier would accept the equipment without the original boxes which had been disposed of who know how many years ago? Back to the computer and another pleasant robot and four more customer representatives, and we are supposed to have a couple of mailing boxes en route along with some mailing labels coming via my e-mail. The jury is out. Nothing in the mail yet. By the time I was finally through with all of this debacle, I was wound tighter than a fiddle string, and you would've thought this media company was coming to take my firstborn. After I shut down the computer, I realized what a mess I was. Had someone pulled my string, I would've buzzed right through the ceiling like a toy top.

The house was quiet. No noise of any kind, so I headed to my favorite chair and closed my eyes. It was past time to bring the emotions and stress level back down, and I knew the next few minutes would be spent with my Maker seeking his peace, and he delivered. The rest of the day was calm with no more drama. Sometimes I wonder why the simplest things become so hard. What have we done to ourselves? This whole transaction with the company should've taken about ten minutes with all of today's technology, yet it took hours. Maybe I needed to practice more patience and kindness and humility, which I really had tried to do. So why was I so frustrated? This wasn't how my day was supposed to go, and I felt like I was being stubbornly pulled along the ground by a horse. Lesson learned, sometimes being kind and flexible happens for a reason. Maybe those robots and customer representatives found someone that wasn't going to yell at them and who was trying to be patient and kind. I was calm on the outside, but boiling on the inside, yet I tried to be on my best behavior. These representatives were victims of the job circumstances, and I have been in their shoes. Not always a very pleasant place to be. Being right isn't nearly as important as being loving and kind and humble. Hopefully my attitude has grown a little more. Trying to be more like him and today, being a little more patient and flexible. The day will be perfectly fine, because I know who is ordering my steps.

*T*he wonder of it all, the majestic mountains, the oceans that can be as quiet and still as glass, yet within a second will roar with waves climbing high. A tiny baby bird ready to take its first flight. Someone coming to faith in him because he saw the way other folks were living in peace and with joy. Leaves that know when to turn color and then dry on the limb and drop off the tree. All of these events fill me with wonder. What an incredulous design our creator has put into place. Yet the top of my "wonder" list will always be that he created me for a purpose and you too. God doesn't make accidents. He sometimes surprises, but we are here for a reason, and despite the way I behave and let him down, he still loves me and welcomes me. How refreshing is that? Then to allow his own Son to take my punishment for my mistakes? There will never be another love so great. Continuing to thank him with our lives and the way we live daily and our service to others because of Him. Thankful to be able to ponder the wonder of it all.

Several weeks ago, that still small voice I hear spoke to me and caught my attention once again. The thought came to mind that I needed to be more aware of how many times I used the word "I" in my conversations with other people. So I started paying attention to my visits with others and doing a mental tally of just how many times I referred to myself in passing conversations. I was astounded and challenged. Then when our pastor started his sermon this past week, guess what his question was? No need to guess. "How often do you use "I" in your conversations?" It wasn't hard to figure out what my Maker had been trying to get through to me for the past week, that's for sure. So how do I change the focus off myself? I want no glory. All the glory goes to him. Looks like I need to get over myself. A challenging reminder that when I glory in my accomplishments, I'm leaving out the most important part. Without him, "I" can do nothing. My work is cut out for me. He knows exactly what I do and think every day. I don't need to plead my case for any other's approval. When all that matters when all is said and done is what did "I" do for him? A fresh start on a new day, to glorify him. A better perspective. Move me out of the way, Lord.

*A*nticipation. That tingle of excitement that can raise goose bumps on the hair at the back of your neck, waiting and knowing that something good or exciting is about to happen. The thought of Christmas Eve night and knowing that in the morning there will be one gift with your name on it under the tree. You're not quite sure what it may be, but trying to imagine raises your anticipation level. Waiting and watching for a spectacular sunrise or sunset, a highly anticipated eclipse, or waiting for a new baby to arrive all involve anticipation. Waiting for a momma moose to return and appear in the marsh like she has done before and is apt to appear again. Half the fun in all these situations in the anticipation.

Many years ago, the disciples were told to work and stay busy yet always with a spirit of anticipation waiting on Christ's return. I think that is a good reminder always. Even though we are busy and working hard, we should be about anticipating his return and watching and listening. He said he would come back and take us to our heavenly home. I believe it. No one knows when, but that doesn't matter. There's going to come a day. Maybe today, pump up the excitement quotient in your day, an occasional glance to heaven listening and watching for his return. Anticipation never felt better.

*F*requently, I wonder where the common art of good manners has gone? Please and thank you are words that are so appreciated, and a little respect and kindness just make the world a little more pleasant, yet sometimes it appears we've forgotten what we've been taught in the "me first" give me give me take take world. Just about the time I'm ready to expound yet again, I look in the mirror, and the reflection I see is staring back at me. I'm guilty too. Out of the blue last night, I remembered a prayer request that I had lifted up to my Maker several months ago, and it was miraculously answered. Yet I had brushed this request to the side and never thanked the one that answered.

I felt a bit ashamed of myself, so today I put my attitude of gratitude back in place and took the time to be thankful all day. This morning, I put my feet on the floor and stood up without an ache or pain. My breakfast was wonderful and the coffee aromatic. We take so much for granted. Today, may we stop and take the time to be thankful and offer up some praise that is so overdue. Take a moment sometime today to say thanks to him and those around you. In everything, give thanks.

*O*nce in a while, I watch a baseball game in the summertime. I really enjoyed watching our children play ball when they were young. When the batter hits that ball as far as his swing will allow, what is his goal? His goal is to get to home plate and score before someone tags him out. Everyone jumps up from the bleachers and fist bumps and high fives each other as the score just inched up another notch and a player came home. We have a favorite walking spot, and our goal is always to get back to the truck we arrived in when our walk is done. Our favorite place to walk is an old airport with many trails that make for smooth and easy walking, and the trails wind around for a long ways. Sometimes, we get to walking, and enjoying it so much, we get farther away from the truck than we ever intended. And when the fussy knees and hip joints start to ache and warn us we're about done, we turn around and head back, but sometimes we can't see the truck; we are so far away. We begin to wonder if we will ever arrive back to where the truck is, which is our goal when we begin our walk. Sometimes it's good to ponder our eternal home, our final destination. There will be a manufacturer's recall one day, and you and I will be reclaimed. Do you and I know where we will land? Our travel can get busy here on earth, and working and raising a family keep us on the run, and then sometimes our circumstances are just plain tough. Might be a good idea to keep heaven in the windshield in front of you. You and I can make it. Perseverance is available. Our Maker would delight in helping you and me along the journey. We merely need to ask. He has gone ahead of us. Cleared the trail. Given us his guidance in his word. Are you ready to arrive home when your days are done? Heaven waits.

*A*s we were drinking coffee in the living room this morning, the subject of irrigation came up. I can't say that I give irrigation much thought on a day-to-day basis, but if I look around and pay attention to the scenery I pass every day, there are irrigation pivots not too far from here where we live, and when we cross the plains, we see evidence of irrigation everywhere. The driest or barest of land is enabled to produce a crop when it has the right amount of nutrients and life-giving water. Sometimes when we ourselves go through those bare, dry trying times, maybe we should remember that we are needing a drink of his living water and some solid food from his word. All of a sudden, we begin to function much better, and the desert we found ourselves in isn't so formidable any more. Our desert might even begin to show signs of life and bloom. Just a reminder that we are never too far gone. He can bring us back to life. The best well spring you will ever find.

"*R*ed rover, red rover, send Susie on over." Do you remember playing this game on the playground as a child? Yes, it dates me, and I wonder how many children today would have a clue as to what game I am talking about? Do you remember how strong some of the kids were who linked arms to keep you from breaking through the human chain link? Did you try to break through the line where you thought the weaklings were and would drop arms from the force of your body crashing into their arms? You knew if you tried to run through the line where the stronger kids were, you would just glance off their linked arms and have to go back to where you started from and try again. This morning, as I picked up my index card that holds the names of so many loved ones with heavy health concerns and prayer requests, I felt helpless. Yet the thought came to mind that no matter how helpless I felt, God would still hear and answer. It's just not up to me to schedule the answers, and with the same thought, I pondered the strength of many praying for the same requests, and I was encouraged. There is strength in numbers. Where two or more are gathered praying and believing, great answers come. Chain link fences are strong, and when we become the strong prayer links that cover our friends and loved ones in prayer, amazing things happen. He is faithful, and he will answer. Once again, the best place to be is close to his heart, in the prayers of many.

$\mathcal{M}$y feet hit the floor extra early this morning, and as I looked out the east bedroom window, I stopped in my tracks. Sunrise doesn't get any prettier. The colors of blues and pinks mixed with gray and orange. Something no human with paint brush in hand can adequately re-create. No camera could fully capture. For just a moment, there was no noise on the busy road behind the cabin. The robins were still quiet. And in that moment, I could hear the words "Be still and know that I am God."

So many dear friends facing seemingly monumental challenges, young and old alike. Political discord was quiet. Agendas dashed. And it was a precious moment to just stand in his presence and take in the surroundings that he created. To breathe deeply of the pine scent. To be thankful. What a beautiful way to start the day and end the day. Be still and know. He is still in control. He hasn't moved. He's right there beside you no matter what you are going through or how far you've wandered. Today, for just a moment, take time to be still in his presence and know.

One of my favorite pastimes with our young sprite this summer has been playing with modeling clay. We made banquets and feasts, ran a taco wagon, made valentine cookies, and fed the world with modeling clay food. As I was modeling some of the clay today, I realized this activity was almost cathartic. I was calm and peaceful, and I was struck by something very evident. When you put the clay away for the day, if you put the clay in some kind of container with a lid that seals the container, generally the next day, the clay is still easy to mold. It remains pliable and in good shape for another use. However, if you don't store the clay properly, it dries out, and when you try to mold it, it breaks and cracks as there is no moisture left in the clay. A very good example of what happens to us, when we pull away from our Maker. As long as we keep our relationship going with him, stay in contact daily, it is a bit easier to allow him to mold us and shape us. We remain a bit more pliable and flexible. If we pull away for any length of time and do life on our own terms, we begin to forget what we've learned, and we may develop some cracks in our armor that aren't easy to patch. Of course, he can restore us and make us like new again. It isn't always a pleasant process yet doable. Maybe it would be a bit easier to just stay in touch and allow him to take the reign. Starting and ending the day with a bit of thanks, taking a moment throughout the day to correspond with him.

Days become a bit more easy and pleasant. Without him, I can do nothing. Letting him do the molding truly is the best way to do life.

"*H*e's got the whole world in his hands." Are you humming that tune yet? A beloved chorus about the greatness of our Maker's love. The whole world. That concept frankly blows my mind. Seven billion people give or take a few. That's a lot of people to care for, yet he cares for each as if he or she is his only child. Back to school season, have you watched your child, neighbor, niece, or nephew step onto the school bus for the first time? Have you watched that child, now as a grown adult, drive out of the driveway for a life in college? Maybe moving to a new town for a new job? Taking flight to whatever his call is? As that child's parent, did you have to swallow hard, maybe shed a tear or a thousand as that child left home? That's an inkling of how much our creator loves each of us. The whole world. As his Son trudged up a long, rocky hill, for each of us. I wonder if God wept to see his Son tormented, abused, and discarded. His life for yours and mine, yet as he was nailed to a cross, this precious Son loved the thief hanging beside him and assured him that today this thief would have eternal life, because he believed. Just one more soul, and he still waits for us to accept him. That all may know the glory of eternal life. That's when real life begins, the day you accept him and his gift of eternal life. If you haven't given the Son of God much thought, maybe today would be a good day to take a few moments to ponder. The thief on the cross. The terrorist that repents and accepts the Son of God. The wayward child that comes back home. The whole world. Calvary covers it all. And I am so thankful on every day of my life.

*T*his summer we have had a family of marmots living in close proximity to our cabin. They started out living on a rock bank behind the cabin, but as inquisitive little ones are, they frequently came for a visit at the wood pile right off the back deck, and there were six of the little fuzzy creatures. Marmots are relatives to a ground hog, only a little longer and leaner, a bit shorter in stature. Their legs are very short, so they are low slung and remind you of a stuffed weasel when they run along the ground. After the sun warmed the rock pile and the early morning dew vanished, we would hear them chirping to notify each other of their various locations in the tall grass behind the cabin. Kind of a hide and seek with noise. One of their favorite spots was on a cement drainage tube that runs beneath our road not far from the cabin. We would see them standing on their hind feet rather like a meerkat keeping an eye on all the surroundings. Summer has given way to fall, and little ones grow up and leave the nest, so for many weeks we haven't seen the marmots, except for one little guy in the past few days which has come back to his former digs for a visit. About midmorning, we see him beside the road, and at noon we see him sitting like the king of the mountain on the wood pile, and he is wearing so much winter fur that he looks like a fuzzy basketball when he sits up. Otherwise, you have to look for the white tip of his nose to know he's not a chunk of wood. Yesterday afternoon, as I was reading on the back deck, I heard the familiar chirping. Couldn't see the little guy, but he was very vocal. Yet no one answered his calls, and his chirps became very sad, almost lonesome sounding. I felt sorry for the little guy. It wasn't long before the chirping stopped, and he was gone. Have you and I ever felt that alone? You and I are crying out for help, yet no one can hear us. Our hearts are troubled, but there are no shoulders to cry on or ears to listen. We appear to be the only glass bottle floating on the ocean surface.

Take heart. You and I are never truly alone. There is someone who is always "with" us. Mention his name, and he is listening right there beside you. He understands the tears and the hurts and the disappointments we face. No matter what you are going through, he is the epitome of love, and he knows about giving it all. The next time you feel all alone, look to heaven. Whisper his name, and let his love invade your very soul. His comfort is the best, and he's waiting.

*H*edgehogs intrigue me and so do porcupines, snails, turtles, and hermit crabs. They carry their homes and protection on the outside, and if danger threatens, they can crawl right into their shells or throw a few well-aimed needles, curl up into a prickly little ball, and nothing messes with them. Yet they all have very vulnerable soft spot. Some of us are a lot like these amusing creatures. Maybe we don't carry our houses on our backs or have an automatic dart response, well at least on most days. Some of us have developed some crust around us or very thick skin over our hearts. Yet remove all that self-made protection, and our soft spots shine through. Just the way our creator made us. We have feelings and show deep emotion. If hurt or abused very much, we, too, are capable of crawling deep down inside ourselves, and those around us never really see who we are for fear we will get injured again. Some of the toughest acting folks I've met have hearts of gold that would do anything for you, yet they hide behind a gruff exterior to guard their hearts, and we are supposed to keep our hearts from allowing the wrong things around us, become part of us, but it's OK to show your soft tender side. Fearfully and wonderfully made with feeling. Eyes of compassion. Ears willing to listen. Hands willing to touch. Maybe today we should try to let others see that we have real, tender hearts too. And if you've been hurt too many times, take those hurts to your Maker, lay them at his feet, and let him dispose of them. Then leave them there. Helping those around us carry their heavy suitcases of pain, putting a little heart into our daily living, serving Him.

$\mathcal{A}$sk any child if they would like a present, and before you finish your sentence, they will excitedly answer yes! If I offered you a dollar, just because I like you, you would probably say, "Well thanks." If I offered you one hundred dollars, just because I could, you would probably say a big thanks! If I offered you a million dollars, how would you react? You probably wouldn't believe me, coupled with what's the catch?

I recently heard a pastor explain this. When someone offers us a huge gift, just because, we are uncomfortable, because we haven't done anything to earn it, we are not worthy, and we imagine that we will probably be obligated all the days of our lives if we accept such a gift. I fear this same thinking keeps some from accepting Christ. It is hard to imagine a man that would give his life for every wrong I've ever done, just because he loves me so much, and all I have to do is accept him and be forgiven. No strings attached. The load of guilt is abolished. He has poured his bottle of white out on our ugliness in the form of grace, and we are as white as snow before him. Don't allow this amazing gift to hold you away just because you can't imagine that kind of love. He made you. He cares for you and every detail of your life, and he waits for you to accept him, forever changed in him.

*W*hat does the word "bravery" make you think of? Robin Hood swinging through the trees in the forest looking for robbers? Taking your newly sharpened hoe to the snake that is trying to gain access to your front door? Walking across a glass catwalk when you are scared out of your wits of high places? Taking a seat in the chemo room ready to slay your giant? Marching single file into a courtyard with other believers like yourself ready to be slain?

We can always imagine what we would do in life and death situations, but I wonder how many of us would be so brave if the time actually came? As I was reading the Bible this morning, the soldiers were coming to get Jesus, and he knows who they are, what they want, and what's ahead. Yet he steps out before them as asks the soldiers who they are looking for?

The soldiers step back and fall on the ground.

He asks them a second time, "Who are you looking for?"

This time as far as I can tell, the soldiers stayed upright. Seems to me this would be a perfect time for everyone to run. Say to a boat on the lake's shore and paddle quickly to the middle. To be guilty of a crime and to take your punishment is one thing, but to be totally blameless and take the punishment for others so that they wouldn't have to be punished put a whole new spin on things. I fear I'm not so brave. So when others around us honestly don't understand why we celebrate Easter and all the events leading to. maybe it's time for us to show a little love to them, the kind of love that accepts them right where they are, unconditionally. If we believe we have been shown a love that knows no bounds, can we do any less? The world needs to see Jesus. The cross loomed before him. Yet he didn't run and hide. Here am I. Send me. No other act of selfless love will ever compare.

"*I* will lift up my eyes unto the hills from which comes my strength." Take a look at the mountains, the big tall ones. Pretty impressive, and they look like they can't be moved. They have withstood the test of time. Wind and weather slowly make changes in their appearance, yet they don't go anywhere, well generally. Many years ago a mountain did move, and a big chunk of it slid into a lake causing all kinds of devastation, and you can still see the scars. Yet the remains of that mountain look strong and solid. Like my Maker's love, it is strong and solid. He will never leave me nor forsake me. I may slide away, but He will remain. Today if your hope quotient seems to have disappeared, take a moment and reconnect with him. He is the solid rock, the cornerstone, and the strong tower, and you can put your trust and faith in him. His word is good. Standing firm. No sliding with him.

*E*arly today, someone asked me to snip what my mom would call a "raveling" from her sleeve. This little one trusted me enough to cut the little string off of her sleeve with a pair of scissors while her arm was in the sleeve. She knew I wouldn't hurt her, and she was stoic, so it took less than a second. Once in a while, I come unraveled, obtain some ragged edges, and begin to fray. I've learned to trust my Maker enough to allow him to do some trimming. When my edges get a bit shaggy and frayed. When I'm feeling less that myself I turn to Him. And in the process after he does the trimming, I pray that I may look a little more like him and unravel in his presence. He can trim the shagginess, the frayed ends off, and give you new insight for the journey. The best trimmer ever.

$\mathcal{W}$e use a lot of onions in our cooking. Once in a while though, we get a little over zealous at the store, and we don't eat all the onions quite as fast as we thought we would when we purchased them, and we end up buying too many. Case in point, there is an onion growing, sitting on the laminated countertop in the kitchen. It has no soil or water and is just basically growing on air, but it is beautiful with thick green tops shooting up about ten inches or so, and it grows rapidly, seemingly overnight. Every day I notice a change in it and ponder how much longer it will grow without any soil or nutrients. Likewise we visited our favorite ten-story tall water falls this past week. Almost in the middle of the river below the falls, there is a bush growing in the river. It actually looks like an ash tree in bush form. Yet we are high above it when we see it, so we can't get an accurate picture of how tall it is or how it survives in the rushing frigid water. We've probably looked at that bush many times this summer but never "saw" the bush until its color changed to golden and a friend pointed it out to us. Which brings me to a question. How often do we look at something yet don't really see? The beautiful snow-capped mountains that are beginning to glisten in the sun. The trees are changing color, and their colors are vibrant. The beautiful clear streams that run constantly. The hurting neighbor that feels like they are surviving only on air. The child sitting by himself in the lunchroom that needs a friend. Once in a while, it is good to slow down for a few minutes and look and see with our hearts. There are many who appear to just be surviving and could really use some help along the way, enriching other's soil so that they can really grow, sharing a few moments a cup of coffee, a batch of cookies, and a smile. We are so blessed, and he enables us to see the beauty and the need around us. Maybe we need to pay attention a little more closely, loving our neighbors as ourselves.

*W*hen tempted, no one should say, "God is tempting me." For God cannot be tempted by evil nor does he tempt anyone, but each person is tempted when they are dragged away by their own evil desire and enticed.

The past week, the age-old question of why do bad things happen to good people cropped up yet again, and how I wish I had a box of "pat" answers so that I could whip out a card that says this is why this problem exists, yet I don't. I struggle with the atrocities of this world also. Why innocent babies are born with cancer or a heart problem, elderly lose their thinking powers, shootings, whatever. These atrocities break my heart. I do not understand, and I am as puzzled as the next guy. Then on the flip side, some of our problems come from our own poor choices. Not my words but his as reflected in the scripture above. We all have our stories, our painful journeys. It is certainly not my job or anyone else's to place judgment or look down on anyone whose struggles are different than mine. I am guilty of making wrong choices too. Whoever made the statement that we are free to make our own decisions, but we aren't free from the consequences, was spot on. So how do we reconcile all of this wondering and pondering? I rely on the verse that says, "I will be with you even until the end of the age." I take comfort that my journey may be uncomfortable, but with him by my side, I have a companion that never fails. He will remain by my side, if I will just ask. Struggles that just happen or self-made struggles. He can cover them. It's truly your call. He will answer.

*O*ver the years, I've formed some of my own personal theology based on his word. Just when I think I have my beliefs all lined up in an orderly fashion and securely in place, someone comes along with a statement or a sermon that crunches my toes and makes me rethink my stance. The realization that my mind-set is harsh and too small makes me cringe. Over the past year, like everyone else, I have watched an influx of people from all over the world coming into our country. I find it overwhelming. I ponder how we are ever going to care for these souls and why are they here? Then I see a statue in a harbor welcoming all in. The tired, the weary, the huddled masses. I see souls who need help, and "whys and wherefores" really don't matter. If someone in our community or state or country needs help, then we best be about taking care of their needs to the best of our ability. Our caring doesn't just stop at the border of our country. We are taught to be going into "all" the world. Overwhelmed yet? There is always something we can do, wherever we are, to help, to serve, to love. Prayers for the persecuted, a Christmas box for a child, a love offering to dig a well, or maybe, just maybe, hopping on a plane and going to help were the need is great. There was a cross on a hill that still beckons us today, and the ground below it is level. There are no stipulations when you arrive at that spot. It doesn't matter why or how you got there. The baggage you carry doesn't matter either. He cares for you and welcomes each of us to come at his bidding. When crowds followed him unmercifully, he never turned anyone away or interrogated them with a bevy of questions. He looked on them just as he looks at us, with compassion, and he welcomed them to come sit at his feet and learn loving all, without qualifications or stipulations, just leaving the details to him. We are called to be his hands and feet. May we love with our whole hearts, always. Can we do any less?

"Though the mountains be shaken and the hills be removed, yet my unfailing love for you will not be shaken nor my covenant of peace be removed," says the Lord who has compassion on you.

These words of scripture are endeared into my very soul. The times when my life has felt like a landslide. He has faithfully been at my side, and his unfailing love has held me steadfast in the palm of his hand. In the summer, we live not far from where a mountain slid into a river many years ago, and tragically many lives were lost. However, there is the beginning of new growth on this mountain scarp now. A few trees here and there are growing, and the jagged edges of the mountain scar are beginning to soften. A vivid reminder that he is right there in the midst of our mess, and he will give us peace in the circumstances of life if we accept it. I am thankful that his word remains ever unchanging, solid as a mountain, and when our world feels like we are crumbling, his love is solid, and his peace is there for the taking.

*H*ow well do you know the people around you? We have lots of friends, and then there are folks we "know of," and we recognize their names. We haven't spent much one-on-one time with them, yet we recognize these folks when we see them. We don't know them well enough to imagine how they will react to various situations. So in order to really get acquainted, we need to spend some one-on-one quality time with them. Then we also have the blessing of meeting total strangers and getting acquainted with them wherever we go. In most cases, it merely takes a smile to start the conversation. There are also longtime friends that we've spent a lot of concentrated time with, and we feel that we know each other really well, yet there is always something new to learn about one another. Which brings me to ask, how well do you know your Maker? Do you know him well, or do you just know "of him?" You've been to church once or twice, maybe heard a television or radio program, or have seen something on the computer about God. How well does he know you? Do you talk to each other frequently? Do you spend some time studying his word so you can learn more about him? Friendships are a two-way street with involvement from both sides, and they are so worth the effort. The more time you spend with him, the better you will get to know him, and like our friendships here on earth, what a blessing to find a real, true friend. You will never find a more loyal or faithful friend. He is always with you, he loves you unequivocally no matter how far you stray away, and he will always be waiting for you return, whenever. Maybe it would be a better idea to just stay in touch. I've found a friend. Oh what a friend.

About the Author

This book is not about me. It is about the moments that he has met me in the most ordinary or not so ordinary everyday life events and shed a little insight. I had the blessing of growing up in a home with both parents that were believers, and they took me to church regularly. When I was eight, I attended membership classes and was baptized. After I was baptized, I sat in the pew, and when communion was passed, I realized that something about me had changed, and as a small girl, tears streamed down my cheeks. Fast forward, my husband and I married right out of high school and laughingly joke that we were engaged in kindergarten, growing up in the same community, riding the same school bus. We have three children and are all over the world, literally. My passion is serving wherever I am needed, and I give him all the glory. As long as there is breath in me, I hope to be able to wear out and not rust out in a rocking chair on the porch. You will find me in Arizona, Africa, Montana, and Missouri, depending on the season. My hobbies are music, quilting, bird watching, and a plethora of other things. Most of all, it is my prayer to honor him in all that I do.

CPSIA information can be obtained
at www.ICGtesting.com
Printed in the USA
LVHW030750210919
631813LV00006B/75